Color of Darkness

Color of Darkness

ELEVEN STORIES AND A NOVELLA

JAMES PURDY

GREENWOOD PRESS, PUBLISHERS
WESTPORT, CONNECTICUT

Library of Congress Cataloging in Publication Data

Purdy, James.
    Color of darkness.

    Reprint of the ed. published by New Directions, New
York.
    I. Title.
[PZ4.P9853Co8] [PS3531.U426] 813'.5'4   74-26739
ISBN 0-8371-7874-6

Acknowledgments for permission to reprint: to the
University of Nebraska Press (*Prairie Schooner*)
and *Mademoiselle* for "You Reach for Your Hat";
to *Black Mountain Review* for "Sound of Talking"; to Robert Williams and *Creative Writing* for
"A Good Woman"; and to *Evergreen Review* for
"Cutting Edge."

Originally published in 1957 by New Directions Books,
New York.

Reprinted with the permission of New Directions Publish-
ing Corporation.

Reprinted in 1975 by Greenwood Press
A division of Congressional Information Service, Inc.
88 Post Road West, Westport, Connecticut 06881

Library of Congress catalog card number 74-26739
ISBN 0-8371-7874-6

Printed in the United States of America

10 9 8 7 6 5 4 3

FOR

DAME EDITH SITWELL

IN

ENGLAND

AND

JULES ARVID

AND

OSBORN ANDREAS

IN

AMERICA

Contents

Color of Darkness

SOMETIMES he thought about his wife, but a thing had begun of late, usually after the boy went to bed, a thing which *should* have been terrifying but which was not: he could not remember now what she had looked like. The specific thing he could not remember was the color of her eyes. It was one of the most obsessive things in his thought. It was also a thing he could not quite speak of with anybody. There were people in the town who would have remembered, of course, what color her eyes were, but gradually he began to forget the general structure of her face also. All he seemed to remember was her voice, her warm hearty comforting voice.

Then there was the boy, Baxter, of course. What did he know and what did he not know. Sometimes Baxter seemed to know everything. As he hung on the edge of the chair looking at his father, examining him closely (the boy never seemed to be able to get close enough to his father), the father felt that Baxter might know everything.

"Bax," the father would say at such a moment, and stare into his own son's eyes. The son looked exactly like the father. There was no trace in the boy's face of anything of his mother.

"Soon you will be all grown up," the father said one night, without ever knowing why he had said this, saying it without his having even thought about it.

"I don't think so," the boy replied.

"Why don't you think so," the father wondered, as surprised by the boy's answer as he had been by his own question.

The boy thought over his own remark also.

"How long does it take?" the boy asked.

"Oh a long time yet," the father said.

1

"Will I stay with you, Daddy," the boy wondered.

The father nodded. "You can stay with me always," the father said.

The boy said *Oh* and began running around the room. He fell over one of his engines and began to cry.

Mrs. Zilke came into the room and said something comforting to the boy.

The father got up and went over to pick up the son. Then sitting down, he put the boy in his lap, and flushed from the exertion, he said to Mrs. Zilke: "You know, I am old!"

Mrs. Zilke laughed. "If you're old, I'm dead," she said. "You must keep your youth," she said almost harshly to the father, after a pause.

He looked up at her, and the boy suddenly moved in his father's arms, looking questioningly at his father. He kissed his father on his face.

"He's young yet," the boy said to Mrs. Zilke.

"Why, of course. He's a young man," she said. "They don't come no younger for fathers."

The father laughed and the boy got up to go with Mrs. Zilke to his bed.

The father thought about Mrs. Zilke's remark and he listened as he heard her reading to the boy from a story-book. He found the story she read quite dry, and he wondered if the boy found anything in it at all.

It was odd, he knew, that he could not remember the color of his wife's eyes. He knew, of course, that he must remember them, and that he was perhaps unconsciously trying to forget. Then he began to think that he could not remember the color of his son's eyes, and he had just looked at them!

⸙   ⸙

"What does he know?" he said to Mrs. Zilke when she came downstairs and sat down for a moment with the newspaper. She lit a cigarette and blew out some smoke before she replied to him. By then he was looking out the window as though he had forgotten her presence and his question.

"He knows everything," Mrs. Zilke said.

The father came to himself now and looked at her gently.

"They all do now, don't they," the father said, meaning children.

"It seems so," the woman said. "Yes," she said, thinking. "They know everything."

"Everybody seems forty years old to me," the father said. "Even children maybe. Except they are complete mysteries to me. I don't know what to say to any of them. I don't know what they know, I guess."

"Oh, I understand that. I raised eight kids and I was always thinking the same thing."

"Well, that relieves me," he told Mrs. Zilke.

She smiled, but in her smile he thought he saw some thought reserved, as though she had not told everything.

"Of course we never know any other human being, do we?" he told Mrs. Zilke, hesitating as though to get the quotation right.

She nodded, enjoying her cigarette.

"Your son is lonely," she said suddenly.

The father did not look at her now.

"I mean by that," she went on, "it's too bad he's an only child."

"Doesn't he have other children over here, though. I thought—"

"Oh, it's not the same," Mrs. Zilke said. "Having in other youngsters like he does on Saturday and all. It's not enough."

"Of course I am gone a good deal."

"You're gone all the time," she said.

"That part can't be helped, of course. You see," he laughed, "I'm a success."

Mrs. Zilke did not return his laughter, he noticed, and he had noticed this before in plain strong old working women of her kind. He admired Mrs. Zilke tremendously. He was glad she had not laughed with him.

"No one should have just the one child," she told him.

"You know," he said, confidentially, "when you have just your work, as I do, people get away from you."

He looked at the bottle of brandy on the bookshelf.

"Would you have a pony of brandy with me, Mrs. Zilke."

She began to say no because she really didn't like it, but there was such a pleading look on his young face, she nodded rather regally, and he got up and poured two shots.

"Thank you for drinking with me," he said suddenly, as though to brush away something that had come between his words and his memory.

"Quite a bouquet," she said, whiffing first.

"You are really very intelligent," he told Mrs. Zilke.

"Because I know the bouquet," she said coldly.

"Oh, that and a lot of other things."

"Well, I don't know anything," Mrs. Zilke said.

"You know everything," he remarked. "All I have is my work."

"That's a lot. They need you," she said.

He sat down now, but he did not touch the brandy, and Mrs. Zilke having smelled the bouquet put her tiny glass down too.

They both sat there for a moment in silence as though they were perhaps at communion.

"I can't remember the color of my wife's eyes," he said, and he looked sick.

Mrs. Zilke sat there as though considering whether this had importance, or whether she might go on to the next topic of their talk.

"And tonight, would you believe it, I couldn't remember the color of his!"

"They're blue as the sea," Mrs. Zilke said rather gruffly, but with a kind of heavy sad tone also in her voice.

"But what does it matter about those little things," she said. "You're an important man!"

He laughed very loud at this, and Mrs. Zilke suddenly laughed too. A cord of tension had been snapped that had existed between them earlier.

The father lifted his glass and said the usual words and Mrs. Zilke took her glass with a slight bored look and sipped.

"I can taste the grapes in that, all right," she said.

"Well, it's the grapes of course I buy it for," he replied in the tone of voice he might have used in a men's bar.

"You shouldn't care what color their eyes are or were," Mrs. Zilke said.

"Well, it's my memory about people," he told her. "I don't know people."

"I know you don't," she said. "But you have other things!"

"No, I don't. Not really. I could remember people if I wanted to."

"If you wanted to," Mrs. Zilke said.

"Well, why can't I remember my wife's eyes," he brought the whole thing out. "Can you remember," he wanted to know, "the color of eyes of all those in your family."

"All forty-two of them," she laughed.

"Well, your husband and your sons and daughters."

"Oh, I expect I can," she was rather evasive.

"But you do, Mrs. Zilke, you know you do!"

"All right, but I'm just a woman about the house. You're out in the world. Why should you know the color of people's eyes! Good grief, yes!"

She put her glass down, and picked up some socks she had been darning before she had put the boy to bed.

"I'm going to work while we talk," she said with a firmness that seemed to mean she would be talking less now and that she would probably not drink the brandy.

Then suddenly closing his own eyes tight he realized that he did not know the color of Mrs. Zilke's eyes. But suddenly he could not be afraid anymore. He didn't care, and he was sure that Mrs. Zilke would not care if he knew or not. She would tell him not to care. And he remembered her, which was, he was sure, more important. He remembered her kindness to him and his son, and how important they both were to him.

⟡   ⟡

"How old *are* you?" Baxter asked him when he was sitting in his big chair with his drink.

"Twenty-eight, I think," the father said vaguely.

"Is that old enough to be dead?" the son wondered.

"Yes and no," the father replied.

"Am I old enough to be dead?"

"I don't think so," the father replied slowly, and his mind was on something else.

"Why aren't we all dead then?" the son said, sailing a tiny paper airplane he had made. Then he picked up a bird he had made out of brown paper and sailed this through the air. It hit a philodendron plant and stuck there in it, as though it were a conscious addition.

"You always think about something else, don't you?" the boy said, and he went up and stared at his father.

"You have blue eyes," the father said. "Blue as the sea."

The son suddenly kissed his father, and the father looked at him for a long time.

"Don't look funny like that," the boy said, embarrassed.

"Like what?" the father said, and lowered his gaze.

The son moved awkwardly, grinding his tiny shoes into the carpet.

"Like you didn't know anything," the boy said, and he ran out into the kitchen to be with Mrs. Zilke.

↑   ↑

After Mrs. Zilke went to bed, which was nearly four hours after the boy had gone, the father was accustomed to sit on downstairs thinking about the problems in his work, but when he was at home like this he often thought about *her*, his wife of long ago. She had run off (this was almost the only term he used for her departure) so long ago and his marriage to her had been so brief that it was almost as though Baxter were a gift somebody had awarded him, and that as the gift increased in value and liability, his own relation to it was more and more ambiguous and obscure. Somehow Mrs. Zilke seemed more real to him than almost anybody else. He could not remember the color of her eyes either, of course, but she was quite real. She was his "mother," he supposed. And the boy was an infant "brother" he did not know too well, and who asked hard questions, and his "wife," who had run off, was just any girl he had gone out with. He could not remember her now at all.

He envied in a way Mrs. Zilke's command over everything. She understood, it seemed, everything she dealt with, and she remembered and could identify all the things which came into her view and under her jurisdiction. The world for her, he was sure, was round, firm, and perfectly illuminated.

For him only his work (and he remembered she had called him a man of importance) had any real meaning, but its meaning to everything else was tenuous.

As he went upstairs that night he looked into his son's room. He was surprised to see that the boy was sleeping with an enormous toy crocodile. The sight of the toy rather shocked him. For a moment he hesitated whether or not to remove the toy and then deciding not to disturb him, he went to his room, took off all his clothes, and stood naked, breathing in front of the opened window. Then he went quickly to bed.

❡ ❡

"It's his favorite doll," Mrs. Zilke said at breakfast. "He wouldn't part with it for the world." She referred to the toy crocodile.

"I would think it would give him nightmares," the father said.

"He don't have nightmares," Mrs. Zilke said, buttering the toast. "There you are, sir!" and she brought him his breakfast.

The father ate silently for a while.

"I was shocked to see that crocodile in his bed," he told Mrs. Zilke again.

"Well, that's something in you, is all," she said.

"I expect. But why couldn't it have been a teddy bear or a girl doll."

"He has those too. It just happened to be crocodile night last night," Mrs. Zilke said, restless now in the kitchen.

"All right," the father said, and he opened the newspaper and began to read about Egypt.

"Your boy needs a dog," Mrs. Zilke said without warning, coming in and sitting down at the table with him. Her hands still showed the traces of soap suds.

"What kind?" the father said.

"You're not opposed to it, then?" Mrs. Zilke replied.

"Why would I oppose a dog." He continued to look at the newspaper.

"He's got to have something," Mrs. Zilke told him.

"Of course," the father said, swallowing some coffee. Then, having swallowed, he stared at her.

"You mean he doesn't have anything?"

"As long as a parent is living, any parent, a child has something. No, I didn't mean *that*," she said without any real apology, and he expected, of course, none.

"I'd rather have him sleeping with a dog now than that crocodile."

"Oh, that," Mrs. Zilke said, impatient.

Then: "All right, then," he said.

He kept nodding after she had gone out of the room. He sat there looking at his old wedding ring which he still wore. Suddenly he took the ring off his finger for the first time since he had had it put on there by the priest. He had left it on all these years simply because, well, he wanted men to think he was married, he supposed. Everybody was married, and he had to be married somehow, anyhow, he knew.

But he left the wedding ring lying on the table, and he went into the front room.

"Sir," Mrs. Zilke called after him.

"Just leave the ring there," he said, thinking she had found it.

But on her face he saw something else. "You'll have to take the boy to buy the dog, you know. I can't walk on hard pavements any more, remember."

"That will be fine, Mrs. Zilke," he said, somehow relieved at what she said.

✓   ✓

The dog they bought at the shop was a small mongrel with a pitifully long tail, and—the father looked very close: brown eyes. Almost the first thing he did was to make a puddle near the father's desk. The father insisted on cleaning it up, and Baxter watched, while Mrs. Zilke muttered to herself in the kitchen. She came in finally and poured something white on the spot.

The dog watched them too from its corner, but it did not seem to want to come out to them.

"You must make up to your new little friend," the father said.

Baxter stared but did not do anything.

"Go to him," the father said, and the son went over into the corner and looked at the pup.

The father sat down at his desk and began to go through his papers.

"Did you have a dog?" Baxter asked his father.

The father thought there at the desk. He did not answer for a long time.

"Yes," the father finally said.

"What color was it," the son asked, and the father stirred in his chair.

"That was so long ago," he said almost as though quoting himself.

"Was it gray then?" the boy wanted to know.

The father nodded.

"A gray dog," the son said, and he began to play with his new pet. The dog lifted its wet paw and bit the boy mildly, and the boy cried a little.

"That's just in fun," the father said absentmindedly.

Baxter ran out into the kitchen, crying a little, and the small dog sat in the corner.

"Don't be afraid of the little fellow now," Mrs. Zilke said. "Go right back and make up to him again."

Baxter and Mrs. Zilke came out of the kitchen and went up to the dog.

"You'll have to name him too," Mrs. Zilke said.

"Will I have to name him, Daddy?" the boy said.

The father nodded.

After supper all three sat in the front room. Baxter nodded a little. The father sat in the easy chair smoking his pipe, the pony of brandy near him. They had gathered here to decide what name to choose for the dog, but nobody had any ideas, it seemed, and the father, hidden from them in a halo of expensive pipe smoke, seemed as far away as if he had gone to the capital again.

Baxter nodded some more and Mrs. Zilke said, "Why, it still isn't bedtime and the little man is asleep!"

From below in the basement where they had put the pup they could all hear the animal's crying, but they pretended not to notice.

Finally, Mrs. Zilke said, "When he is housebroken you can sleep with him, Baxter."

Baxter opened his eyes and looked at her. "What is that?" he said.

"When he learns to take care of himself, not make puddles, you can have him in bed with you."

"I don't want to," the boy said.

Mrs. Zilke looked stoically at the father.

"Why don't you want to, sweetheart," she said, but her words showed no emotion.

"I don't want anything," the boy said.

Mrs. Zilke looked at the father again, but he was even more lost to them.

"What's that hanging loose in your mouth." Mrs. Zilke suddenly sprang to attention, adjusting her spectacles, and looking at the boy's mouth.

"This." The boy pointed to his lips, and blushed slightly. "Gum," he said.

"Oh," Mrs. Zilke said.

The clock struck eight.

"I guess it *is* your bedtime," Mrs. Zilke said.

She watched the boy.

"Do you want to go to bed, Baxter," she said, abstractedly.

The boy nodded.

"Say goodnight to daddy and kiss him," she told him perfunctorily.

The boy got up and went over to his father, but stopped in front of the rings of smoke.

"Goodnight," the boy lisped.

"What's that in his mouth," the father addressed his remark to Mrs. Zilke and his head came out of the clouds of smoke.

Mrs. Zilke got up painfully now and putting on her other glasses looked at the boy.

"What are you sucking?" Mrs. Zilke said, and both of them now stared at him.

Baxter looked at them as though they had put net about him. From his long indifference to these two people a sudden new feeling came slowly into his dazed, slowly moving mind. He moved back a step, as though he wanted to incite them.

"Baxter, sweetheart," the old woman said, and both she and the father stared at him as though they had found out perhaps who he was.

"What do you have in your mouth, son," the father said, and the word *son* sounded queer in the air, moving toward the boy with the heaviness and suggestion of nausea that the dog puddle had given him earlier in the afternoon.

"What is it, son," the father said, and Mrs. Zilke watched him, her new understanding of the boy written on her old red face.

"I'm chewing gum," the boy told them.

"No, you're not now, Baxter. Why don't you tell us," Mrs. Zilke whined.

Baxter went over into the corner where the dog had been.

"That dog is bad, isn't he," Baxter giggled, and then he suddenly laughed loudly when he thought what the dog had done.

Meanwhile Mrs. Zilke and the father were whispering in the cloud of tobacco smoke.

Baxter sat down on the floor talking to himself, and playing with a broken piece of Tinker Toy. From his mouth still came sounds of something vaguely metallic.

Then Mrs. Zilke came up stealthily, a kind of sadness and kindness both in her face, like that of a trained nurse.

"You can't go to sleep with that in your mouth, sweetheart."

"It's gum," the boy said.

Mrs. Zilke's bad legs would not let her kneel down beside the boy on the floor as she wished to do. She wanted to have a close talk with him, as she did sitting by his bed in the nursery, but instead now, standing over him, so far away, her short heavy breathing sounding obnoxiously in the room, she said only, "You've never lied to me before, Baxter."

"Oh yes I have," Baxter said. "Anyhow this is gum," and he made the sounds again in his mouth.

"I'll have to tell your father," she said, as though *he* were already away in Washington.

"It's gum," the boy said in a bored voice.

"It's metal, I think," she said looking worriedly at the boy.

"It's just gum." The boy hummed now and played with the Tinker Toy.

"You'll have to speak to him," Mrs. Zilke said.

The father squatted down with the son, and the boy vaguely realized this was the first time the father had ever made the motion of playing with him. He stared at his father, but did not listen to what he was talking about.

"If I put my finger in your mouth will you give it to me?" the father said.

"No," the boy replied.

"You wouldn't want to swallow the thing in your mouth," the father said.

"Why not," the boy wondered.

"It would hurt you," the father told him.

"You would have to go to the hospital," Mrs. Zilke said.

"I don't care where I go," the boy said. "It's a toy I have in my mouth."

"What sort of toy," the father wondered, and he and Mrs. Zilke suddenly became absorbed in the curiosity of what Baxter had there.

"A golden toy," the boy laughed, but his eyes looked glassy and strange.

"Please," the father said, and he put his finger gently on the boy's lips.

"Don't touch me!" the son called out suddenly. "I hate you!"

The father drew back softly as though now he would return to his work and his papers, and it was Mrs. Zilke who cried out instead: "Shame!"

"I do hate him," the boy said. "He's never here anyhow."

"Baxter," the father said.

"Give your father what's in your mouth or you will swallow it and something terrible will happen to you."

"I want it right where it is," the boy said, and he threw the Tinker Toy at Mrs. Zilke.

"Look here now, Baxter," the father said, but still sleepily and with no expression.

"Shut your goddamn face," the boy spat out at his father.

The father suddenly seized the boy's chin and jaw and forced him to spit out what he had.

His wedding ring fell on the carpet there, and they all stared at it a second.

Without warning the son kicked the father vigorously in the groin and escaped, running up the stairs.

Baxter stopped deliberately from the safety of the upper staircase and pronounced the obscene word for his father as though this was what he had been keeping for him for a long time.

Mrs. Zilke let out a low cry.

The father writhing in pain from the place where the boy had kicked him, managed to say with great effort: "Tell me where he learned a word like that."

Mrs. Zilke went over to where the ring lay now near the Tinker Toy.

"I don't know what's happening to people," she said, putting the ring on the table.

Then, a weary concern in her voice, she said, "Sir, are you hurt?"

The tears fell from the father's eyes for having been hit in such a delicate place, and he could not say anything more for a moment.

"Can I do anything for you, sir?" Mrs. Zilke said.

"I don't think right now, thank you," he said. "Thank you." He grunted with the exquisite pain.

"I've put your ring up here for safekeeping," she informed him.

The father nodded from the floor where he twisted in his pain.

You May Safely Gaze

"Do we always have to begin on Milo at these Wednesday lunches," Philip said to Guy. Carrying their trays, they had already picked out their table in the cafeteria, and Philip, at least, was about to sit down.

"Do *I always* begin on Milo?" Guy wondered, surprised.

"You're the one who knows him, remember," Philip said.

"Of course, Milo is one of the serious problems in our office, and it's only a little natural, I suppose, to mention problems even at one of our Wednesday lunches."

"Oh, forget it," Philip said. Seated, he watched half-amused as Guy still stood over the table with his tray raised like a bus-boy who will soon now move away with it to the back room.

"I don't dislike Milo," Guy began. "It's not that at all."

Philip began to say something but then hesitated, and looked up at the cafeteria clock that showed ten minutes past twelve. He knew, somehow, that it was going to be Milo all over again for lunch.

"It's his attitude not just toward his work, but life," Guy said, and this time he sat down.

"His life," Philip said, taking swift bites of his chicken à la king.

Guy nodded. "You see now he spares himself the real work in the office due to this physical culture philosophy. He won't even let himself get mad anymore or argue with me because that interferes with the development of his muscles and his mental tranquillity, which is so important for muscular development. His whole life now he says is to be strong and calm."

"A muscle ascetic," Philip laughed without amusement.

"But working with him is not so funny," Guy said, and

15

Philip was taken aback to see his friend go suddenly very pale. Guy had not even bothered to take his dishes off his tray but allowed everything to sit there in front of him as though the lunch were an offering he had no intention of tasting.

"Milo hardly seems anybody you and I could know, if you ask me," Guy pronounced, as though the final decision had at last been made.

"You forget one of us *doesn't*," Philip emphasized again, and he waved his fork as though they had finally finished now with Milo, and could go on to the real Wednesday lunch.

But Guy began again, as though the talk for the lunch had been arranged after all, despite Philip's forgetfulness, around Milo.

"I don't think he is even studying law anymore at night, as he was supposed to do."

"Don't tell me that," Philip said, involuntarily affecting concern and half-resigning himself now to the possibility of a completely wasted hour.

"Oh, of course," Guy softened his statement, "I guess he goes to the law library every night and reads a little. Every waking hour is, after all, not for his muscles, but every real thought, you can bet your bottom dollar, *is*."

"I see," Philip said, beginning on his pineapple snow.

"It's the only thing on his mind, I tell you," Guy began again.

"It's interesting if that's the only thing on his mind, then," Philip replied. "I mean," he continued, when he saw the black look he got from Guy, "—to know somebody who is obsessed . . ."

"What do you mean by that?" Guy wondered critically, as though only he could tell what it was that Milo might be.

"You said he wanted to devote himself to just this one thing." Philip wearily tried to define what he had meant.

"I tried to talk to Milo once about it," Guy said, now deadly serious, and as though, with all preliminaries past, the real part of his speech had begun. Philip noticed that his friend had still not even picked up his knife or fork, and his food must be getting stone cold by now. " 'Why do you want to look any stronger,' I said to Milo. He just stared at me, and I said, 'Have you ever taken a good look in the mirror the way you are now,' and he just smiled his sour smile again at me. 'Have you ever looked, Milo?' I said, and even I had to laugh when I repeated my own question, and he kind of laughed then too . . . Well, for God's sake, he knows after all that nobody but a few freaks are going to look like he looks, or will look, if he keeps this up. You see he works on a new part of his body every month. One month he will be working on his pectorals, the next his calf muscles, then he will go in for a period on his latissimus dorsi."

Philip stopped chewing a moment as though seeing these different muscle groups slowly developing there before him. Finally, he managed to say, "Well at least he's interested in something, which is more than . . ."

"Yes, he's interested in *it*, of course," Guy interrupted, "—what he calls being the sculptor of his own body, and you can find him almost any noon in the gym straining away while the other men in our office do as they please with their lunch hour."

"You mean they eat their lunch then." Philip tried humor.

"That's right," Guy hurried on. "But he and this Austrian friend of his who also works in my office, they go over to this gym run by a cripple named Vic somebody, and strain their guts out, lifting barbells and throwing their arms up and around on benches, with dumbbells in their fists, and come back an hour later to their work looking as though they had been in a rock mixer. They actually stink of gym, and several of the stenographers have complained saying they always know when it's exercise day all right. But nothing stops those boys, and they just take all the gaff with as much good humor as two such egomaniacs can have."

"Why egomaniacs, for God's sake," Philip wondered, putting his fork down with a bang.

"Well, Philip," Guy pleaded now. "To think of their own bodies like that. These are not young boys, you know. They must be twenty-five or so, along in there, and you would think they would begin to think of other people, other people's bodies, at least." Guy laughed as though to correct his own severity before Philip. "But no," he went on. "They have to be Adonises."

"And their work suffers?" Philip wondered vaguely, as though, if the topic had to be continued, they might now examine it from this aspect.

"The kind of work young men like them do—it don't matter, you know, if you're good or not, nobody knows if you're really good. They do their work and get it out on time, and you know their big boss is still that old gal of seventy who is partial to young men. She sometimes goes right up to Milo, who will be sitting at his desk relaxed as a jellyfish, doing nothing, and she says, 'Roll up your sleeves, why don't you, and take off your necktie on a warm day like this,' and it will be thirty degrees outside and cool even in the office. And Milo will smile like a four-year-old at her because he loves admiration more than anything in the world, and he rolls up his sleeves and then all this bulge of muscle comes out, and the old girl looks like she'd seen glory, she's that gone on having a thug like that around."

"But you sound positively bilious over it," Philip laughed.

"Philip, look," Guy said with his heavy masculine patience, "doesn't it sound wrong to you, now seriously?"

"What in hell do you mean by wrong, though?"

"Don't be that way. You know goddamn well what I mean."

"Well, then, no, I can't say it is. Milo or whatever his name."

"You know it's Milo," Guy said positively disgusted.

"Well, he is, I suppose, more typical than you might think from the time, say, when you were young. Maybe there weren't such fellows around then."

"Oh there were, of course."

"Well, now there are more, and Milo is no exception."

"But he looks at himself all the time, and he has got himself tattooed recently and there in front of the one mirror in the office, it's not the girls who stand there, no, it's Milo and this Austrian boy. They're always washing their hands or combing their hair, or just looking at themselves right out, not sneaky-like the way most men do, but like some goddamn chorus girls. And oh, I forgot, this Austrian fellow got tattooed too because

Milo kept after him, and then he was sorry. It seems the Austrian's physical culture instructor gave him hell and said he had spoiled the appearance of his deltoids by having the tattoo work done."

"Don't tell me," Philip said.

Guy stared as he heard Philip's laugh, but then continued: "They talked about the tattoo all morning, in front of all the stenogs, and whether this Austrian had spoiled the appearance of his deltoid muscles or not."

"Well, it *is* funny, of course, but I couldn't get worked up about it the way you are."

"They're a symbol of the new America and I don't like it."

"You're terribly worked up."

"Men on their way to being thirty, what used to be considered middle age, developing their bodies and special muscles and talking about their parts in front of women."

"But they're married men, aren't they?"

"Oh sure," Guy dismissed this. "Married and with kids."

"What more do you want then. Some men are nuts about their bowling scores and talk about that all the time in front of everybody."

"I see you approve of them."

"I didn't say that. But I think you're overreacting, to use the phrase . . ."

"You don't have to work with them," Guy went on. "You don't have to watch them in front of the one and only office mirror."

"Look, I've known a lot of women who griped me because they were always preening themselves, goddamn narcissists too. I don't care for narcissists of either sex."

"Talk about Narciss-uses," said Guy. "The worst was last summer when I went with Mae to the beach, and there *they* were, both of them, right in front of us on the sand."

Philip stiffened slightly at the prospect of more.

"Milo and the Austrian," Guy shook his head. "And as it was Saturday afternoon there didn't seem to be a damn place free on the beach and Mae wanted to be right up where these

Adonises or Narciss-uses, or whatever you call them, were. I said, 'We don't want to camp here, Mae,' and she got suddenly furious. I couldn't tell her how those birds affected me, and they hardly even spoke to me either, come to think about it. Milo spit something out the side of his mouth when he saw me, as though to say *that for you.*"

"That was goddamn awful for you," Philip nodded.

"Wait till you hear what happened, for crying out loud. I shouldn't tell this during my lunch hour because it still riles me."

"Don't get riled then. Forget them."

"I have to tell you," Guy said. "I've never told anybody before, and you're the only man I know will listen to a thing like this. . . . You know," he went on then, as though this point were now understood at last between them, "Mae started staring at them right away. 'Who on earth are they?' she said, and I couldn't tell whether she was outraged or pleased, maybe she was a bit of both because she just fixed her gaze on them like paralyzed. 'Aren't you going to put on your sun tan lotion and your glasses?' I said to her, and she turned on me as though I had hit her. 'Why don't you let a woman relax when I never get out of the house but twice in one year,' she told me. I just lay back then on the sand and tried to forget they were there and that she was there and that even I was there."

Philip began to light up his cigarette, and Guy said, "Are you all done eating already?" and he looked at his own plate of veal cutlet and peas which was nearly untouched. "My God, you are a fast eater. Why, do you realize how fast you eat," he told Philip, and Philip said he guessed he half-realized it. He said at night he ate slower.

"In the bosom of your family," Guy laughed.

Philip looked at the cafeteria clock and stirred unceremoniously.

"But I wanted to finish telling you about these boys."

"Is there *more?*" Philip pretended surprise.

"Couldn't you tell the way I told it there was," Guy said, an indeterminate emotion in his voice.

"I hope nothing happened to Mae," Philip offered weakly.

"Nothing ever happens to Mae," Guy dismissed this impatiently. "No, it was them, of course. Milo and the Austrian began putting on a real show, you know, for everybody, and as it was Saturday afternoon, as I said, nearly everybody from every office in the world was there, and they were all watching Milo and the Austrian. So, first they just did the standard routine, warm-ups, you know, etc., but from the first every eye on the beach was on them, they seemed to have the old presence, even the life guards were staring at them as though nobody would ever dare drown while they were carrying on, so first of all then they did handstands and though they did them good, not good enough for that many people to be watching. After all somebody is always doing handstands on the beach, you know. I think it was their hair attracted people, they have very odd hair, they look like brothers that way. Their hair is way too thick, and of course too long for men of our generation. . . ."

"Well, how old do you think I am?" Philip laughed.

"All right, of *my* generation, then," Guy corrected with surliness. He went on, however, immediately: "I think the reason everybody watched was their hair, which is a peculiar kind of chestnut color, natural and all that, but maybe due to the sun and all their exercising had taken on a funny shade, and then their muscles were so enormous in that light, bulging and shining with oil and matching somehow their hair that I think that was really what kept people looking and not what they did. They didn't look quite real, even though in a way they are the style.

"I kept staring, and Mae said, 'I thought you wasn't going to watch,' and I could see she was completely held captive by their performance as was, I guess, everybody by then on the goddamn beach.

" 'I can't help looking at freaks,' I told Mae, and she gave me one of her snorts and just kept looking kind of bitter and satisfied at seeing something like that. She's a great woman for sights like that, she goes to all the stock shows, and almost every nice Sunday she takes the kids to the zoo. . . ."

"Well, what finally did come off?" Philip said, pushing back his chair.

"The thing that happened, nobody in his right mind would ever believe, and probably lots of men and boys who saw it happen never went home and told their families."

"It should have been carried in the papers then," Philip said coolly and he drank all of his as yet untouched glass of water.

"I don't know what word I would use to describe it," Guy said. "Mae has never mentioned it to this day, though she said a little about it on the streetcar on the way home that afternoon, but just a little, like she would have referred to a woman having fainted and been rushed to the hospital, something on that order."

"Well, for Pete's sake now, what did happen?" Philip's ill humor broke forth for a moment, and he bent his head away from Guy's look.

"As I said," Guy continued quietly, "they did all those more fancy exercises then after their warm ups, like leaping on one another's necks, jumping hard on each other's abdomens to show what iron men they were, and some rough stuff but which they made look fancy, like they threw one another to the sand as though it was a cross between a wrestling match and an apache dance, and then they began to do some things looked like they were out of the ballet, with lots of things like jumping in air and splits, you know. You know what kind of trunks that kind of Narciss-uses wear, well these were tighter than usual, the kind to make a bullfighter's pants look baggy and oversize, and as though they had planned it, while doing one of their big movements, their trunks both split clear in two, at the same time, with a sound, I swear, you could have heard all over that beach.

"Instead of feeling at least some kind of self-consciousness, if not shame, they both busted out laughing and hugged one another as though they'd made a touchdown, and they might as well both been naked by now, they just stood there and looked down at themselves from time to time like they were alone in the shower, and laughed and laughed, and an old woman next to them just laughed and laughed too, and all Mae did was look once and then away with a funny half-smile on her mouth, she didn't show any more concern over it than the next one.

Here was a whole beach of mostly women, just laughing their heads off because two men no longer young, were, well, exposing themselves in front of everybody, for that's all it was."

Philip stared at his empty water glass.

"I started to say something to Mae, and she nearly cut my head off, saying something like *why don't you mind your own goddamn business* in a tone unusually mean even for her. *Don't look damn you if you don't like it* was what my own wife said to me.

Suddenly Philip had relaxed in his chair as though the water he had drunk had contained a narcotic. He made no effort now to show his eagerness to leave, to hurry, or to comment on what was being said, and he sat there staring in the direction of, but not at, Guy.

"But the worst part came then," Guy said, and then looking critically and uneasily at Philip, he turned round to look at the cafeteria clock, but it showed only five minutes to one, and their lunch hour was not precisely over.

"This old woman," he continued, swallowing hard, "who had been sitting there next to them got out a sewing kit she had, and do you know what?"

"I suppose she sewed them shut," Philip said sleepily and still staring at nothing.

"That's exactly correct," Guy said, a kind of irritated disappointment in his voice. "This old woman who looked at least eighty went right up to them the way they were and she must have been a real seamstress, and before the whole crowd with them two grown men laughing their heads off she sewed up their tights like some old witch in a story, and Mae sat there as cool as if we was playing bridge in the church basement, and never said boo, and when I began to really let off steam, she said *Will you keep your big old ugly mouth shut or am I going to have to hit you over the mouth with my beach clogs.* That's how they had affected my own wife."

"So," Guy said, after a pause in which Philip contributed nothing, "this country has certainly changed since I grew up in it. I said that to Mae and that was the final thing I had to say on the subject, and those two grown men went right on lying there on the sand, every so often slapping one another on their muscles, and combing their hair with oil, and laughing all the time, though I think even they did have sense enough not to get up and split their trunks again or even they must have known they would have been arrested by the beach patrol."

"Sure," Philip said vacantly.

"So that's the story of Milo and the Austrian," Guy said.

"It's typical," Philip said, like a somnambulist.

"Are you sore at me or something," Guy said, picking up his and Philip's checks.

"Let me pay my own, for Christ's sake," Philip said.

"Listen, you *are* sore at me, I believe," Guy said.

"I have a rotten headache is all," Philip replied, and he picked up his own check.

"I hope I didn't bring it on by talking my head off."

"No," Philip replied. "I had it since morning."

Don't Call Me by My Right Name

HER new name was Mrs. Klein. There was something in the meaning that irritated her. She liked everything about her husband except his name and that had never pleased her. She had fallen in love with him before she found out what his name was. Once she knew he was Klein, her disappointment had been strong. Names do make a great difference, and after six months of marriage she found herself still not liking her name. She began using more and more her maiden name. Then she always called herself on her letters Lois McBane. Her husband seldom saw the mail arrive so perhaps he did not know, and had he known she went by her old name he might not have cared enough to feel any particular hurt.

Lois Klein, she often thought as she lay next to her husband in bed. It is not the name of a woman like myself. It does not reflect my character.

One evening at a party when there had been more drinking for her than usual, she said offhand to him in the midst of some revelry: "I would like you to change your name."

He did not understand. He thought that it was a remark she was making in drink which did not refer to anything concrete, just as once she had said to him, "I want you to begin by taking your head off regularly." The remark had meant nothing, and he let it pass.

"Frank," she said, "you must change your name, do you hear? I cannot go on being Mrs. Klein."

Several people heard what it was she said, and they laughed loudly so that Lois and Frank would hear them appreciating the remark.

"If you were all called Mrs. Klein," she said turning to the men who were laughing, "you would not like to be Mrs. Klein either."

Being all men, they laughed harder.

"Well, you married him, didn't you," a man said, "and we guess you will have to keep his name."

"If he changed his name," another of the men said, "what name would you have him change it to?"

Frank put his hand on her glass, as though to tell her they must go home, but she seized the glass with his hand on it and drank quickly out of it.

"I hadn't thought what name I did want," she said, puzzled.

"Well, you aren't going to change your name," Frank said. "The gentlemen know that."

"The gentlemen do?" she asked him. "Well, I don't know what name I would like it changed to," she admitted to the men.

"You don't look much like Mrs. Klein," one of the men said and began to laugh again.

"You're not friends!" she called back at them.

"What are we, then?" they asked.

"Why don't I look like Mrs. Klein?" she wanted to know.

"Don't you ever look in the mirror?" one of the men replied.

"We ought to go, Lois," her husband said.

She sat there as though she had heard the last of the many possible truths she could hear about herself.

"I wonder how I will get out of here, Frank," she said.

"Out of where, dear?" he wondered. He was suddenly sad enough himself to be dead, but he managed to say something to her at this point.

"Out of where I seem to have got into," she told him.

The men had moved off now and were laughing among themselves. Frank and Lois did not notice this laughter.

"I'm not going to change my name," he said, as though to himself. Then turning to her: "I know it's supposed to be wrong to tell people when they're drunk the insane whim they're having is insane, but I am telling you now and I may tell the whole room of men."

"I have to have my name changed, Frank," she said. "You know I can't stand to be tortured. It is too painful and I am not young anymore. I am getting old and fat."

"No wife of mine would ever be old or fat," he said.

"I just cannot be Mrs. Klein and face the world."

"Anytime you want me to pull out is all right," he said. "Do you want me to pull out?"

"What are you saying?" she wanted to know. "What did you say about pulling out?"

"I don't want any more talk about your changing your name or I intend to pull up stakes."

"I don't know what you're talking about. You know you can't leave me. What would I do, Frank, at my age?"

"I told you no wife of mine is old."

"I couldn't find anybody now, Frank, if you went."

"Then quit talking about changing our name."

"*Our* name? I don't know what you mean by *our* name."

He took her drink out of her hand and when she coaxed and whined he struck her not too gently over the mouth.

"What was the meaning of that?" she wanted to know.

"Are you coming home, Mrs. Klein?" he said, and he hit her again. Her lip was cut against her teeth so that you could see it beginning to bleed.

"Frank, you're abusing me," she said, white and wide-eyed now, and as though tasting the blood slightly with the gin and soda mix.

"Mrs. Klein," he said idiotically.

It was one of those fake dead long parties where nobody actually knows anybody and where people could be pushed out of windows without anybody's being sure until the morrow.

"I'm not going home as Mrs. Klein," she said.

He hit her again.

"Frank, you have no right to hit me just because I hate your name."

"If you hate my name what do you feel then for me? Are you going to act like my wife or not."

"I don't want to have babies, Frank. I will not go through that at my age. Categorically not."

He hit her again so that she fell on the floor, but this did not seem to surprise either her or him because they both continued the conversation.

"I can't make up my mind what to do," she said, weeping a little. "I know of course what the safe thing is to do."

"Either you come out of here with me as Mrs. Klein, or I go to a hotel room alone. Here's the key to the house," he said, and he threw it on the floor at her.

Several of the men at the party had begun to notice what was really going on now. They thought that it was married clowning at first and they began to gather around in a circle, but what they saw had something empty and stiff about it that did not interest and yet kept one somehow watching. For one thing, Mrs. Klein's dress had come up and exposed her legs, which were not beautiful.

"I can't decide if I can go on with his name," she explained from the floor position to the men.

"Well, it's a little late, isn't it, Mrs. Klein," one of the men said in a sleepy voice.

"It's never too late, I don't suppose, is it?" she inquired. "Oh, I can't believe it is even though I feel old."

"Well, you're not young," the same man ventured. "You're too old to be lying there."

"My husband can't see my point of view," she explained. "And that is why he can't understand why his name doesn't fit me. I was unmarried too long, I suppose, to suddenly surrender my own name. I have always been known professionally and socially under my own name and it is hard to change now, I can tell you. I don't think I can go home with him unless he lets me change my name."

"I will give you just two minutes," Mr. Klein said.

"For what? Only two minutes for what?" she cried.

"To make up your mind what name you are going out of here with."

"I know, men," she said, "what the sensible decision is, and tomorrow, of course, when I'm sober I will wish I had taken it."

Turning to Frank Klein, she said simply, "You will have to go your way without me."

He looked hurriedly around as though looking for an exit to leave by, and then he looked back to her on the floor as though he could not come to a decision.

"Come to your senses," Frank Klein said unemphatically.

"There were hundreds of Kleins in the telephone directory," she went on, "but when people used to come to my name they recognized at once that I was the only woman going under my own special name."

"For Jesus Christ's sake, Lois," he said, turning a peculiar green color.

"I can't go with you as Mrs. Klein," she said.

"Well, let me help you up," he said.

She managed to let him help her up.

"I'm not going home with you, but I will send you in a cab," he informed her.

"Are you leaving me?" she wanted to know.

He did not know what to say. He felt anything he said might destroy his mind. He stood there with an insane emptiness on his eyes and lips.

Everyone had moved off from them. There was a silence from the phonograph and from the TV set which had both been going at the same time. The party was over and people were calling down to cabs from all the windows.

"Why won't you come home with me?" she said in a whisper.

Suddenly he hurried out the door without waiting for her.

"Frank!" she called after him, and a few of the men from the earlier group came over and joked with her.

"He went out just like a boy, without any sense of responsibility," she said to them without any expression in her voice.

She hurried on out too, not waiting to put her coat on straight.

She stood outside in the fall cold and shivered. Some children went by dressed in Hallowe'en costumes.

"Is she dressed as anybody?" one of the children said pointlessly.

"Frank!" she began calling. "I don't know what is happening really," she said to herself.

Suddenly he came up to her from behind a hedge next to where she was standing.

"I couldn't quite bring myself to go off," he said.

She thought for a minute of hitting him with her purse which she had remembered to bring, but she did nothing now but watch him.

"Will you change your name?" she said.

"We will live together the way we have been," he said not looking at her.

"We can't be married, Frank, with that name between us."

Suddenly he hit her and knocked her down to the pavement.

She lay there for a minute before anything was said.

"Are you conscious?" he said crouching down beside her. "Tell me if you are suffering," he wanted to know.

"You have hurt something in my head, I think," she said, getting up slightly on one elbow.

"You have nearly driven me out of my mind," he said, and he was making funny sounds in his mouth. "You don't know what it means to have one's name held up to ridicule like this. You are such a cruel person, Lois."

"We will both change our names, if you like," she said.

"Why do you torture me?" he said. "Why is it you can't control your power to torture?"

"Then we won't think about it, we will go home," she said, in a cold comforting voice. "Only I think I am going to be sick," she warned.

"We will go home," he said in a stupid voice.

"I will let you call me Mrs. Klein this one evening, then tomorrow we will have a good talk." At the same moment she fell back on the walk.

Some young men from the delicatessen who had been doing

inventory came by and asked if there was anything they could do.

"My wife fell on the walk," he said. "I thought she was all right. She was talking to me just a moment ago."

"Was it your wife, did you say?" the younger man leaned down to look at her.

"Mrs. Klein," Frank replied.

"You are Mr. Klein, then?"

"I don't understand," the older of the two young men said. "You don't look somehow like her husband."

"We have been married six months."

"I think you ought to call a doctor," the younger man said. "She is bleeding at the mouth."

"I hit her at a party," Frank said.

"What did you say your name was?" the older man asked.

"Mr. Klein. She is Mrs. Klein," Frank told them.

The two men from the delicatessen exchanged looks.

"Did you push her?" the one man asked.

"Yes," Frank said. "I hit her. She didn't want to be Mrs. Klein."

"You're drunk," the one man ventured an opinion.

Lois suddenly came to. "Frank, you will have to take me home," she said. "There is something wrong with my head. My God," she began to scream, "I am in awful pain."

Frank helped her up again.

"Is this your husband?" the one man asked.

She nodded.

"What is your name?" he wanted to know.

"It's none of your business," she said.

"Are you Mrs. Klein?" he asked.

"No," Lois replied, "I don't happen to be Mrs. Klein."

"Come on, J. D., we can't get mixed up in this," the younger man said. "Whatever the hell their names are."

"Well, I'm not Mrs. Klein, whoever you are," she said.

Immediately then she struck Frank with the purse and he fell back in surprise against the building wall.

"Call me a cab, you cheap son of a bitch," she said. "Can't you see I'm bleeding?"

Eventide

MAHALA had waited as long as she thought she could; after
all, Plumy had left that morning and now here it was going
on four o'clock. It was hardly fair if she was loitering, but
she knew that certainly Plumy would never loiter on a day
like this when Mahala wanted so to hear. It was in a way
the biggest day of her whole life, bigger than any day she
had ever lived through as a girl or young woman. It was
the day that decided whether her son would come back to
live with her or not.

And just think, a whole month had rolled past since he
left home. Two months ago if anyone would have said that
Teeboy would leave home, she would have stopped dead
in her tracks, it would have been such a terrible thing even
to say, and now here she was, talking over the telephone
about how Teeboy had gone.

"My Teeboy is gone," that is what Mahala said for a
long time after the departure. These words announced to her
mind what had happened, and just as an announcement they
gave some mild comfort, like a pain-killer with a fatal disease.

"My Teeboy," she would say, like the mother of a dead
son, like the mother of a son who had died in battle,
because it hurt as much to have a son missing in peacetime
as to have lost him through war.

The room seemed dark even with the summer sunshine
outside, and close, although the window was open. There
was a darkness all over the city. The fire department had
been coming and going all afternoon. There were so many
fires in the neighborhood — that is what she was saying to

33

Cora on the telephone, too many fires: the fire chief had just whizzed past again. No, she said to Cora, she didn't know if it was in the white section of town or theirs, she couldn't tell, but oh it was so hot to have a fire.

Talking about the fires seemed to help Mahala more than anything. She called several other old friends and talked about the fires and she mentioned that Teeboy had not come home. The old friends did not say much about Teeboy's not having returned, because, well, what was there to say about a boy who had been practicing to leave home for so long. Everyone had known it but her blind mother love.

"What do you suppose can be keeping my sister Plumy?" Mahala said to herself as she walked up and down the hall and looked out from behind the screen in the window. "She would have to fail me on the most important errand in the world."

Then she thought about how much Plumy hated to go into white neighborhoods, and how the day had been hot and she thought of the fires and how perhaps Plumy had fallen under a fire truck and been crushed. She thought of all the possible disasters and was not happy, and always in the background there was the fresh emotion of having lost Teeboy.

"People don't know," she said, "that I can't live without Teeboy."

She would go in the clothes closet and look at his dirty clothes just as he had left them; she would kiss them and press them to her face, smelling them; the odors were especially dear to her. She held his rayon trousers to her bosom and walked up and down the small parlor. She had not prayed; she was waiting for Plumy to come home first, then maybe they would have prayer.

"I hope I ain't done anything I'll be sorry for," she said.

It was then, though, when she felt the worst, that she heard the steps on the front porch. Yes, those were Plumy's steps, she was coming with the news. But whatever the news was, she suddenly felt, she could not accept it.

As she came up the steps, Plumy did not look at Mahala

with any particular kind of meaning on her face. She walked unsteadily, as if the heat had been too much for her.

"Come on in now, Plumy, and I will get you something cool to drink."

Inside, Plumy watched Mahala as if afraid she was going to ask her to begin at once with the story, but Mahala only waited, not saying anything, sensing the seriousness of Plumy's knowledge and knowing that this knowledge could be revealed only when Plumy was ready.

While Mahala waited patiently there in the kitchen, Plumy arranged herself in the easy chair, and when she was once settled, she took up the straw fan which lay on the floor.

"Well, I seen him!" Plumy brought the words out.

This beginning quieted the old mother a little. She closed her mouth and folded her hands, moving now to the middle of the parlor, with an intentness on her face as if she was listening to something high up in the sky, like a plane which is to drop something, perhaps harmless and silver, to the ground.

"I seen him!" Plumy repeated, as if to herself. "And I seen all the white people!" she finished, anger coming into her voice.

"Oh, Plumy," Mahala whined. Then suddenly she made a gesture for her sister to be quiet because she thought she heard the fire department going again, and then when there was no sound, she waited for her to go on, but Plumy did not say anything. In the slow afternoon there was nothing, only a silence a city sometimes has within itself.

Plumy was too faint from the heat to go on at once; her head suddenly shook violently and she slumped in the chair.

"Plumy Jackson!" Mahala said, going over to her. "You didn't *walk* here from the white district! You didn't walk them forty-seven blocks in all this August heat!"

Plumy did not answer immediately. Her hand caressed the worn upholstery of the chair.

"You know how nervous white folks make me," she said at last.

Mahala made a gesture of disgust. "Lord, to think you

walked it in this hot sun. Oh, I don't know why God wants
to upset me like this. As if I didn't have enough to make me
wild already, without havin' you come home in this con-
dition."

Mahala watched her sister's face for a moment with the
same figuring expression of the man who comes to read the
water meter. She saw everything she really wanted to know
on Plumy's face: all her questions were answered for her
there, yet she pretended she didn't know the verdict; she
brought the one question out:

"You did see Teeboy, honey?" she said, her voice changed
from her tears. She waited a few seconds, and then as Plumy
did not answer but only sank deeper into the chair, she
continued: "What word did he send?"

"It's the way I told you before," Plumy replied crossly.
"Teeboy ain't coming back. I thought you knowed from the
way I looked at you that he ain't coming back."

Mahala wept quietly into a small handkerchief.

"Your pain is realer to me sometimes than my own,"
Plumy said, watching her cry. "That's why I hate to say to
you he won't never come back, but it's true as death he
won't."

"When you say that to me I got a feeling inside myself
like everything had been busted and taken; I got the feeling
like I don't have nothing left inside of me."

"Don't I know that feeling!" Plumy said, almost angrily,
resting the straw fan on the arm of the chair, and then
suddenly fanning herself violently so that the strokes sounded
like those of a small angry whip. "Didn't I lose George Watson of sleeping sickness and all 'cause doctor wouldn't
come?"

Plumy knew that Mahala had never shown any interest
in the death of her own George Watson and that it was an
unwelcome subject, especially tonight, when Teeboy's never
coming back had become final, yet she could not help mentioning George Watson just the same. In Mahala's eyes
there really had never been any son named George Watson;

there was only a son named Teeboy and Mahala was the only mother.

"It ain't like there bein' no way out to your troubles: it's the way out that kills you," Mahala said. "If it was goodbye for always like when someone dies, I think I could stand it better. But this kind of parting ain't like the Lord's way!"

Plumy continued fanning herself, just letting Mahala run on.

"So he ain't never coming back!" Mahala began beating her hands together as if she were hearing music for a dance.

Plumy looked away as the sound of the rats downstairs caught her attention; there seemed to be more than usual tonight and she wondered why they were running so much, for it was so hot everywhere.

Her attention strayed back to Mahala standing directly in front of her now, talking about her suffering: "You go through all the suffering and the heartache," she said, "and then they go away. The only time children is nice is when they're babies and you know they can't get away from you. You got them then and your love is all they crave. They don't know who you are exactly, they just know you are the one to give them your love, and they ask you for it until you're worn out giving it."

Mahala's speech set Plumy to thinking of how she had been young and how she had had George Watson, and how he had died of sleeping sickness when he was four.

"My only son died of sleeping sickness," Plumy said aloud, but not really addressing Mahala. "I never had another. My husband said it was funny. He was not a religious man, but he thought it was queer."

"Would you like a cooling drink?" Mahala said absently.

Plumy shook her head and there was a silence of a few minutes in which the full weight of the heat of evening took possession of the small room.

"I can't get used to that idea of him *never* comin' back!" Mahala began again. "I ain't never been able to understand that word *never* anyhow. And now it's like to drive me wild."

There was another long silence, and then, Mahala suddenly rousing herself from drowsiness and the heat of the evening, began eagerly: "How did he look, Plumy? Tell me how he looked, and what he was doing. Just describe."

"He wasn't doin' nothin'!" Plumy said flatly. "He looked kind of older, though, like he had been thinking about new things."

"Don't keep me waiting," Mahala whined. "I been waitin' all day for the news, don't keep me no more, when I tell you I could suicide over it all. I ain't never been through such a hell day. Don't you keep me waitin'."

"Now hush," Plumy said. "Don't go frettin' like this. Your heart won't take a big grief like this if you go fret so."

"It's *so* unkind of you not to tell," she muffled her lips in her handkerchief.

Plumy said: "I told you I talked to him, but I didn't tell you where. It was in a drinking place called the Music Box. He called to me from inside. The minute I looked at him I knew there was something wrong. There was something wrong with his hair."

"With his hair!" Mahala cried.

"Then I noticed he had had it all made straight! That's right," she said looking away from Mahala's eyes. "He had had his hair straightened. 'Why ain't you got in touch with your mother,' I said. 'If you only knowed how she was carryin' on.'

"Then he told me how he had got a tenor sax and how he was playing it in the band at the Music Box and that he had begun a new life, and it was all on account of his having the tenor sax and being a musician. He said the players didn't have time to have homes. He said they were playing all the time, they never went home, and that was why he hadn't been."

Plumy stopped. She saw the tenor sax only in her imagination because he had not shown it to her, she saw it curved and golden and heard it playing far-off melodies. But the real reason she stopped was not on account of the tenor sax but because of the memory of the white woman who had come out just then. The white woman had come out and put her arm around Teeboy. It had made her get creepy all over. It was the first time that Plumy had realized that Teeboy's skin was nearly as light as the white people's.

Both Teeboy and the woman had stood there looking at Plumy, and Plumy had not known how to move away from them. The sun beat down on her in the street but she could not move. She saw the streetcars going by with all the white people pushing one another around and she looked around on the scorched pavements and everyone was white, with Teeboy looking just as white as the rest of them, looking just as white as if he had come out of Mahala's body white, and as if Mahala had been a white woman and not her sister, and as if Mahala's mother and hers had not been black.

Then slowly she had begun walking away from Teeboy and the Music Box, almost without knowing she was going herself, walking right on through the streets without knowing what was happening, through the big August heat, without an umbrella or a hat to keep off the sun; she could see no place to stop, and people could see the circles of sweat that were forming all over her dress. She was afraid to stop and she was afraid to go on walking. She felt she would fall down eventually in the afternoon sun and it would be like the time George Watson had died of sleeping sickness, nobody would help her to an easy place.

Would George Watson know her now? That is what she was thinking as she walked through the heat of that afternoon. Would he know her — because when she had been his mother she had been young and her skin, she was sure, had been lighter; and now she was older looking than she remembered her own mother ever being, and her skin was very black.

It was Mahala's outcries which brought her back to the parlor, now full of the evening twilight.

"Why can't God call me home?" Mahala was asking. "Why can't He call me to His Throne of Grace?"

Then Mahala got up and wandered off into her own part of the house. One could hear her in her room there, faintly kissing Teeboy's soiled clothes and speaking quietly to herself.

"Until you told me about his having his hair straightened, I thought maybe he would be back," Mahala was saying from the room. "But when you told me that, I knew. He won't never be back."

Plumy could hear Mahala kissing the clothes after she had said this.

"He was so dear to her," Plumy said aloud. It was necessary to speak aloud at that moment because of the terrible feeling of evening in the room. Was it the smell of the four o'clocks, which must have just opened to give out their perfume, or was it the evening itself which made her uneasy? She felt not alone, she felt someone else had come, uninvited and from far away.

Plumy had never noticed before what a strong odor the four o'clocks had, and then she saw the light in the room, growing larger, a light she had not recognized before, and then she turned and saw *him*, George Watson Jackson, standing there before her, large as life. Plumy wanted to call out, she wanted to say *No* in a great voice, she wanted to brush the sight before her all away, which was strange because she was always wanting to see her baby and here he was, although seventeen years had passed since she had laid him away.

She looked at him with unbelieving eyes because really he was the same, the same except she did notice that little boys' suits had changed fashion since his day, and how that everything about him was slightly different from the little children of the neighborhood now.

"Baby!" she said, but the word didn't come out from her mouth, it was only a great winged thought that could not be made into sound. "George Watson, honey!" she said still in her silence.

He stood there, his eyes like they had been before. Their beauty stabbed at her heart like a great knife; the hair looked so like she had just pressed the wet comb to it and perhaps

put a little pomade on the sides; and the small face was clean
and sad. Yet her arms somehow did not ache to hold him like
her heart told her they should. Something too far away and
too strong was between her and him; she only saw him as
she had always seen resurrection pictures, hidden from us
as in a wonderful mist that will not let us see our love
complete.

There was this mist between her and George Jackson, like
the dew that will be on the four o'clocks when you pick one
of them off the plant.

It was her baby come home, and at such an hour.

Then as she came slowly to herself, she began to raise herself slightly, stretching her arms and trying to get the words
to come out to him:

"George Watson, baby!"

This time the words did come out, with a terrible loudness,
and as they did so the light began to go from the place where
he was standing: the last thing she saw of him was his bright
forehead and hair, then there was nothing at all, not even
the smell of flowers.

Plumy let out a great cry and fell back in the chair. Mahala
heard her and came out of her room to look at her.

"What you got?" Mahala said.

"I seen *him!* I seen *him!* Big as life!"

"Who?" Mahala said.

"George Watson, just like I laid him away seventeen
years ago!"

Mahala did not know what to say. She wiped her eyes dry,
for she had quit crying.

"You was exposed too long in the sun," Mahala said
vaguely.

As she looked at her sister she felt for the first time the
love that Plumy had borne all these years for a small son
Mahala had never seen, George Watson. For the first time she
dimly recognized Plumy as a mother, and she had suddenly a
feeling of intimacy for her that she had never had before.

She walked over to the chair where Plumy was and laid
her hand on her. Somehow the idea of George Watson's

being dead so long and yet still being a baby a mother could love had a kind of perfect quality that she liked. She thought then, quietly and without shame, how nice it would be if Teeboy could also be perfect in death, so that he would belong to her in the same perfect way as George Watson belonged to Plumy. There was comfort in tending the grave of a dead son, whether he was killed in war or peace, and it was so difficult to tend the memory of a son who just went away and never came back. Yet somehow she knew as she looked at Plumy, somehow she would go on with the memory of Teeboy Jordan even though he still lived in the world.

As she stood there considering the lives of the two sons Teeboy Jordan and George Watson Jackson, the evening which had for some time been moving slowly into the house entered now as if in one great wave, bringing the small parlor into the heavy summer night until you would have believed daylight would never enter there again, the night was so black and secure.

Why Can't They Tell You Why?

PAUL knew nearly nothing of his father until he found the box of photographs on the backstairs. From then on he looked at them all day and every evening, and when his mother Ethel talked to Edith Gainesworth on the telephone. He had looked amazed at his father in his different ages and stations of life, first as a boy his age, then as a young man, and finally before his death in his army uniform.

Ethel had always referred to him as *your father,* and now the photographs made him look much different from what this had suggested in Paul's mind.

Ethel never talked with Paul about why he was home sick from school and she pretended at first she did not know he had found the photographs. But she told everything she thought and felt about him to Edith Gainesworth over the telephone, and Paul heard all of the conversations from the backstairs where he sat with the photographs, which he had moved from the old shoe boxes where he had found them to two big clean empty candy boxes.

"Wouldn't you know a sick kid like him would take up with photographs," Ethel said to Edith Gainesworth. "Instead of toys or balls, old photos. And my God, I've hardly mentioned a thing to him about his father."

Edith Gainesworth, who studied psychology at an adult center downtown, often advised Ethel about Paul, but she did not say anything tonight about the photographs.

"All mothers should have pensions," Ethel continued. "If it isn't a terrible feeling being on your feet all day before the public and then having a sick kid under your feet when

43

you're off at night. My evenings are worse than my days."

These telephone conversations always excited Paul because they were the only times he heard himself and the photographs discussed. When the telephone bell would ring he would run to the backstairs and begin looking at the photographs and then as the conversation progressed he often ran into the front room where Ethel was talking, sometimes carrying one of the photographs with him and making sounds like a bird or an airplane.

Two months had gone by like this, with his having attended school hardly at all and his whole life seemingly spent in listening to Ethel talk to Edith Gainesworth and examining the photographs in the candy boxes.

Then in the middle of the night Ethel missed him. She rose feeling a pressure in her scalp and neck. She walked over to his cot and noticed the Indian blanket had been taken away. She called Paul and walked over to the window and looked out. She walked around the upstairs, calling him.

"God, there is always something to bother you," she said. "Where are you, Paul?" she repeated in a mad sleepy voice. She went on down into the kitchen, though it did not seem possible he would be there, he never ate anything.

Then she said *Of course*, remembering how many times he went to the backstairs with those photographs.

"Now what are you doing in here, Paul?" Ethel said, and there was a sweet but threatening sound to her voice that awoke the boy from where he had been sleeping, spread out protectively over the boxes of photographs, his Indian blanket over his back and shoulder.

Paul crouched almost greedily over the boxes when he saw this ugly pale woman in the man's bathrobe looking at him. There was a faint smell from her like that of an uncovered cistern when she put on the robe.

"Just here, Ethel," he answered her question after a while.

"What do you mean, *just here*, Paul?" she said going up closer to him.

She took hold of his hair and jerked him by it gently as though this was a kind of caress she sometimes gave him.

This gentle jerking motion made him tremble in short successive starts under her hand, until she let go.

He watched how she kept looking at the boxes of photographs under his guard.

"You sleep here to be near them?" she said.

"I don't know why, Ethel," Paul said, blowing out air from his mouth as though trying to make something disappear before him.

"You don't know, Paul," she said, her sweet fake awful voice and the stale awful smell of the bathrobe stifling as she drew nearer.

"Don't, don't!" Paul cried.

"Don't what?" Ethel answered, pulling him toward her by seizing on his pajama tops.

"Don't do anything to me, Ethel, my eye hurts."

"Your eye hurts," she said with unbelief.

"I'm sick to my stomach."

Then bending over suddenly, in a second she had gathered up the two boxes of photographs in her bathrobed arms.

"Ethel!" he cried out in the strongest, clearest voice she had ever heard come from him. "Ethel, those are my candy boxes!"

She looked down at him as though she was seeing him for the first time, noting with surprise how thin and puny he was, and how disgusting was one small mole that hung from his starved-looking throat. She could not see how this was her son.

"These boxes of pictures are what makes you sick."

"No, no, Mama Ethel," Paul cried.

"What did I tell you about calling me Mama," she said, going over to him and putting her hand on his forehead.

"I called you Mama Ethel, not Mama," he said.

"I suppose you think I'm a thousand years old." She raised her hand as though she was not sure what she wished to do with it.

"I think I know what to do with these," she said with a pretended calm.

"No, Ethel," Paul said, "give them here back. They are my boxes."

"Tell me why you slept out here on this backstairs where you know you'll make yourself even sicker. I want you to tell me and tell me right away."

"I can't, Ethel, I can't," Paul said.

"Then I'm going to burn the pictures," she replied.

He crawled hurrying over to where she stood and put his arms around her legs.

"Ethel, please don't take them, Ethel. Pretty please."

"Don't touch me," she said to him. Her nerves were so bad she felt that if he touched her again she would start as though a mouse had gotten under her clothes.

"You stand up straight and tell me like a little man why you're here," she said, but she kept her eyes half closed and turned from him.

He moved his lips to answer but then he did not really understand what she meant by *little man*. That phrase worried him whenever he heard it.

"What do you do with the pictures all the time, all day when I'm gone, and now tonight? I never heard of anything like it." Then she moved away from him, so that his hands fell from her legs where he had been grasping her, but she continued to stand near his hands as though puzzled what to do next.

"I look is all, Ethel," he began to explain.

"Don't bawl when you talk," she commanded, looking now at him in the face.

Then: "I want the truth!" she roared.

He sobbed and whined there, thinking over what it was she could want him to tell her, but everything now had begun to go away from his attention, and he had not really ever understood what had been expected of him here, and now everything was too hard to be borne.

"Do you hear me, Paul?" she said between her teeth, very close to him now and staring at him in such an angry way he closed his eyes. "If you don't answer me, do you know what I'm going to do?"

"Punish?" Paul said in his tiniest child voice.

"No, I'm not going to punish this time," Ethel said.

"You're not!" he cried, a new fear and surprise coming now into his tired eyes, and then staring at her eyes, he began to cry with panicky terror, for it seemed to him then that in the whole world there were just the two of them, him and Ethel.

"You remember where they sent Aunt Grace," Ethel said with terrible knowledge.

His crying redoubled in fury, some of his spit flying out onto the cold calcimine of the walls. He kept turning the while to look at the close confines of the staircase as though to find some place where he could see things outside.

"Do you remember where they sent her?" Ethel said in a quiet patient voice like a woman who has endured every unreasonable, disrespectful action from a child whom she still can patiently love.

"Yes, yes, Ethel," Paul cried hysterically.

"Tell Ethel where they sent Aunt Grace," she said with the same patience and kind restraint.

"I didn't know they sent little boys there," Paul said.

"You're more than a little boy now," Ethel replied. "You're old enough. . . . And if you don't tell Ethel why you look at the photographs all the time, we'll have to send you to the mental hospital with the bars."

"I don't know why I look at them, dear Ethel," he said now in a very feeble but wildly tense voice, and he began petting the fur on her houseslippers.

"I think you do, Paul," she said quietly, but he could hear her gentle, patient tone disappearing and he half raised his hands as though to protect him from anything this woman might now do.

"But I don't know why I look at them," he repeated, screaming, and he threw his arms suddenly around her legs.

She moved back, but still smiling her patient, knowing, forgiving smile.

"All right for you, Paul." When she said that *all right for you* it always meant the end of any understanding or reasoning with her.

"Where are we going?" he cried, as she ushered him through the door, into the kitchen.

"We're going to the basement, of course," she replied.

They had never gone there together before, and the terror of what might happen to him now gave him a kind of quiet that enabled him to walk steady down the. long irregular steps.

"You carry the boxes of pictures, Paul," she said, "since you like them so much."

"No, no," Paul cried.

"Carry them," she commanded, giving them to him.

He held them before him and when they reached the floor of the basement, she opened the furnace and, tightening the cord of her bathrobe, she said coldly, her white face lighted up by the fire, "Throw the pictures into the furnace door, Paul."

He stared at her as though all the nightmares had come true, the complete and final fear of what may happen in living had unfolded itself at last.

"They're Daddy!" he said in a voice neither of them recognized.

"You had your choice," she said coolly. "You prefer a dead man to your own mother. Either you throw his pictures in the fire, for they're what makes you sick, or you will go where they sent Aunt Grace."

He began running around the room now, much like a small bird which has escaped from a pet shop into the confusion of a city street, and making odd little sounds that she did not recognize could come from his own lungs.

"I'm not going to stand for your clowning," she called out, but as though to an empty room.

As he ran round and round the small room with the boxes of photographs pressed against him, some of the pictures fell upon the floor and these he stopped and tried to recapture, at the same time holding the boxes tight against him, and making, as he picked them up, frothing cries of impotence and acute grief.

Ethel herself stared at him, incredulous. He not only could not be recognized as her son, he no longer looked like a child, but in his small unmended night shirt like some crippled and dying animal running hopelessly from its pain.

"Give me those pictures!" she shouted, and she seized a few which he held in his fingers, and threw them quickly into the fire.

Then turning back, she moved to take the candy boxes from him.

But the final sight of him made her stop. He had crouched on the floor, and, bending his stomach over the boxes, hissed at her, so that she stopped short, not seeing any way to get at him, seeing no way to bring him back, while from his mouth black thick strings of something slipped out, as though he had spewed out the heart of his grief.

Man and Wife

"How could it happen to you in good times if you didn't do nothing wrong?" Peaches Maud said.

"Peaches, I am trying to tell you," Lafe replied. "None of the men in the plant ever liked me." Then as though quoting somebody: "I am frankly difficult."

"Difficult? You are the easiest-to-get-along-with man in the whole country."

"I am not manly," he said suddenly in a scared voice, as though giving an order over a telephone.

"Not manly?" Peaches Maud said and surprise made her head move back slightly as though the rush of his words was a wind in her face.

"What has manly got to do with you being fired?" She began walking around the small apartment, smoking one of the gold-tipped cigarettes he bought for her in the Italian district.

"The foreman said the men never liked me on account of my character," Lafe went on, as though reporting facts he could scarcely remember about a person nearly unknown to him.

"Oh, Jesus," Maud said, the cigarette hanging in her mouth and a thin stream of smoke coming up into her half-closed eyes. "Well, thank God we live where nobody knows us. That is the only thing comes to mind to be grateful for. And for the rest, I don't know what in hell you are really talking about, and my ears won't let me catch what you seem to be telling."

"I have done nothing wrong, Peaches Maud."

"Did you ever do anything right?" She turned to him with hatred.

"I have no character, Maud," he spoke slowly, as though still quoting from somebody.

It was true, Maud thought, puffing vigorously on the Italian cigarette: he had none at all. He had never found a character to have. He was always about to do something or start something, but not having a character to start or do it with left him always on the road to preparation.

"What did the men care whether you had a character or not?" Maud wanted to know.

For nearly a year now she had worn corsets, but this afternoon she had none, and, it being daylight, Lafe could see with finality how fat she was and what unsurpassed large breasts stuck out from her creased flesh. He was amazed to think that he had been responsible so long for such a big woman. Seeing her tremendous breasts, he felt still more exhausted and unready for his future.

"They told me in the army, Peaches, I should have been a painter."

"Who is this *they?*" she inquired with shamed indignation.

"The men in the mental department."

Lafe felt it essential at this moment to go over and kiss Maud on the throat. He tasted the talcum powder she had dusted herself with against the heat, and it was not unwelcome in his situation. Underneath the talcum he could taste Maud's sweat.

"All right, now." Maud came down a little to him, wiping his mouth free of the talcum powder. "What kind of a painter did these mental men refer to?"

"They didn't mean somebody who paints chairs and houses," Lafe said, looking away so that she would not think he was criticizing her area of knowledge.

"I mean why did they think you was meant for a painter?" Maud said.

"They never tell you those things," he replied. "The tests test you and the mental men come and report the findings."

"Well, Jesus, what kind of work will you go into if it ain't factory work?"

Lafe extricated a large blue handkerchief dotted with white stars and held this before him as though he were waiting for a signal to cover his face with it.

"Haven't you always done factory work?" Peaches Maud summarized their common knowledge in her threatening voice.

"Always, always," he replied in agony.

"Just when you read how the whole country is in for a big future, you come home like this to me," she said, suddenly triumphant. "Well, I can tell you, I'm not going back to that paint factory, Lafe. I will do anything but go back and eat humble pie to Mrs. Goreweather."

"I don't see how you could go back." He stared at her flesh.

"What meaning do you put in those words?" she thundered. Then when he stared at her uncomprehending: "You seem to lack something a husband ought to have for his wife."

"That's what everything seems to be about now," he said. "It's what I lack everywhere."

"Stop that down-at-the-mouth talk," she commanded evenly.

"All the way home on the streetcar I sat like a bedbug." He ignored her.

"Lafe, what have I told you?" She tried to attract his attention now back to herself.

"I have always lacked something and that lack was in my father and mother before me. My father had drink and my mother was easily recognized as . . . ."

She pulled his arm loosely toward her: "Don't bring that up in all this trouble. She was anyhow a mother. . . . Of course, we could never afford for me to be a mother. . . ."

"Maybe I should go back and tell the men all the things I lack they still don't know about."

"You say things that are queer, all right," Maud said in a quieter voice, and then with her old sarcasm: "I can kind of see how you got on the men's nerves if you talked to them like you talk at home."

"You're beginning to see, you say, Peaches?" Lafe said, almost as though he were now the judge himself, and then he began to laugh.

"I wish you would never laugh that way," Maud corrected him. "I hate that laugh. It sounds like some kid looking through a bathroom window. Jesus, Lafe, you ought to grow up."

He continued to laugh for a few moments, giving her the chance to see he had already changed a little for her. It was his laughing that made her pace up and down the room, despite the heat of July, and listen with growing nervousness to the refrigerator make its clattering din.

"I can see what maybe the men meant," she said in her quiet triumph-tone of voice, and at the same time putting rage into her eyes as they stared at the refrigerator.

"Christ, I hated every goddamn man."

"You can't afford to hate nobody! You can't go around hating men like that when you earn your bread with them."

"You hated Mrs. Goreweather."

"Look how unfair! You know Mrs. Goreweather had insanity in her family, and she pounced on me as a persecution target. You never even hinted there was any Mrs. Goreweather character at the factory."

"I was *her!*"

"Lafe, for Jesus' sake, in all this heat and noise, let's not have any of this mental talk, or I will put on my clothes and go out and get on the streetcar."

"I'm telling you what it was. The company psychiatrist told me I was the Mrs. Goreweather of my factory."

"How could he know of her?"

"I told him."

"No," she said stopping dead in the room. "You didn't go and tell him about her!" She picked up a large palm straw fan from a table and fanned with angry movements the large patches of sweat and talcum powder on her immense meaty body. As Lafe watched her move the fan, he thought how much money had gone to keep her in food these seven peculiar years.

"I am not a normal man, Peaches Maud," he said without conviction or meaning. He went over to her and touched her shoulder.

"I'll bet that psychiatrist isn't even married," Maud said, becoming more gentle but suddenly more worried.

"He wasn't old," Lafe said, the vague expression coming over his face again. "He might be younger than me."

"If only that damn refrigerator would shut up," she complained, not knowing now where to turn her words.

She went over to the bed and sat down, and began fanning the air in his direction, as though to calm him or drive away any words he might now say.

"You have no idea how that refrigerator nags me sometimes when you can be gone and away at work. I feel like I just got to go out when I hear it act so."

"Maud," he said, and he stopped her arm from fanning him. "I have never once ceased to care for you in all this time and trouble."

"Well, I should hope," she said, suddenly silly, and fanning her own body now more directly.

"You will always attract me no matter what I am."

"Jesus, Lafe!" And she beat with the fan against the bedpost so that it shook a little.

Then they both noticed that the refrigerator was off.

"Did I jar it still?" she wondered.

But the moment she spoke it began again, louder and more menacing.

"I am not a man to make you happy." Lafe touched her shoulder again.

"I thought I told you I couldn't stand that mental talk. I have never liked having you say you felt like a bug or any other running of yourself down. Just because you lost your job don't think you can sit around here with me in this heat and talk mental talk now."

"Maud, I feel I should go away and think over what it is

I have done to myself. I feel as though everything was beginning to go away from me."

"What in Jesus' name would you go away on?" she exclaimed, and she threw the fan in the direction of the refrigerator.

"I realize now how much of me there is that is not right," he said, as though he had finally succeeded in bringing this fact to his own attention.

"Jesus! Jesus!" she cried. "How much longer do I, an old married woman, have to listen to this?"

"Peaches Maud!" he said, standing up and looking down at her squatting bulk on the bed. "There's no point me postponing telling you. Why I am without a job should be no sort of mystery for you, for you are after all the woman I married. . . . Have you been satisfied with me?"

"Satisfied?" she said, becoming quiet again, and her hand rising as though still in possession of the fan. "Lafe, listen a moment." Peaches spoke quickly, holding her finger to her face, as though admiring a strain of music. "Did you ever hear it go so loud before? I swear it's going to explode on us. Can they explode, do you suppose?"

He stood there, his face and body empty of meaning, not looking where she pointed to the refrigerator.

Maude broke a piece of chewing gum in two and, without offering him the other piece, began to unfold the tin foil and then to chew the gum industriously but with a large frown between her eyes as though she could expect no pleasure from what she had put into her mouth.

"You never let me show you nothing but the outside," he said, his face going white and his eyes more vacant.

"Well, that's all anybody human wants to hear," she shouted, but she felt a terrible excitement inside, and her mouth went so dry she could hardly chew the gum.

"Peaches Maud, you have to listen to what I am trying to tell you." He touched her jaws as though to stop her chewing. "First of all you must answer my first question. Have you been satisfied with me?"

Peaches Maud felt welling up within her for the first time

in seven years a terrible tempest of tears. She could not explain why or from where these tears were coming. She felt also, without warning, cold and she got up and put on her kimono.

"Don't tell me no more now." She faced him, drawing the kimono sash tight about her.

The refrigerator clattered on in short unrhythmic claps as though to annihilate all other sound.

"Answer my question, Peaches." He took her hand up from the folds of the kimono.

"I bought this for you in Chinatown." He made an effort to raise his voice.

"I don't want to hear no memory talks, Lafe, for the love of Christ!" And she looked down at him suddenly as though she had gone up above him on a platform.

"Maud," he coaxed, putting a new and funny hopeful tone into his voice, "I can forget all that mental talk like you say. I did before anyhow. The men in the army tried to make me feel things too, with their tests, and here I went and married you."

"Stop it now," she began to make crying sounds. "I can't bear to hear no more of that talk, I tell you. Put it off for later. I don't feel up to hearing, I tell you."

"We both quick change and make up our minds, don't we?" he said, briefly happy. He kissed her on the face.

"Don't kiss me when I feel like I do," she said peevishly.

Then without any warning, shouting as though something had stung her: "What did the company psychiatrist tell you?"

"You got to answer my first question first," Lafe said, a kind of mechanical strength coming to him.

"I can't answer until I hear what he told you," she said.

"Peaches," he pleaded with her.

"I mean what I said now." She began to sob a little.

"No, don't tell me after all, Lafe." Her face was open now and had a new empty weak quality he had never seen on it before. I feel if it's what I am fearing I'd split open like a stone."

"How could it be that bad?" he seemed to ask himself this question.

"I can tell it is because you keep making it depend on me being satisfied. I know more than you think I know."

Then she began to scream at him again as though to stop any tears that might have force enough to fall.

"What did you do at that factory that wasn't human? Oh, I thank Jesus we don't live in the same neighborhood with them men that work with you. This apartment may be hell with nothing but foreigners around us and that busted refrigerator and no ventilation but heat from the roof, but thank Jesus nobody don't know us."

"You won't answer me, then?" he said, still as calm and empty in his movements as before.

"You're not a woman," she told him, "and you can't understand the first question can't be answered till I know what you done."

"I asked the psychiatrist if it was a crime."

"Well, what did he tell you?" Peaches Maud raised her voice as though she saw ahead some faint indication of escape.

"He said it depended. It was what the men thought where you had to work."

"Well, what in the name of Christ did the men think?"

"They thought it was a crime."

"Was it a boy you was stuck on?" Peaches Maud said, making her voice both empty and quiet, and at the same time all the tears came onto her face as though sprayed there by a tiny machine, in one second.

"Did the psychiatrist call you up, Peaches?" he said, and he took hold of the bedpost and stared away from her.

Then, when she did not answer, he went over to her: "Did he, Peaches?" He took her by the hands and waited for her to answer.

"You leave loose of me, Lafe Krause. Do you hear? Leave loose of my hands."

"Peaches," he called in a voice that seemed to come from under the floor.

"Don't call me that old love name," she wept. "I'm an old fat woman tied down to a . . ."

She waited before she said the word, listening as though for any sound that might perhaps rescue them there both together.

"Did he call you up?" Lafe kept on, but his voice carried now no real demand, and came as though at a still greater distance from under where they stood.

Listening sharply, Maud felt it was true: the refrigerator had stopped again, and the silence was high and heavy as the sky outside.

"Did he call you, Maud, did he?"

"No," she answered, finally, still feeling he had to be addressed at some depth under where she was standing. "It was your mother. She told me before we got married. I said I would take a chance."

"The old bitch told you," he reflected in his exhausted voice.

"Considering the way the son turned out, the mother can hardly be blamed," Maud said, but her voice was equally drained of meaning.

"Peaches," he said, but as if not addressing the word to her at all, and going rapidly over to the refrigerator and opening up the door.

"The little light is out that was on here," he said dully.

"There ain't no point in fussing with it now," she remarked.

"Maybe I could fix it," he said.

"I doubt that. I doubt you could, Lafe Krause. I don't think I would want you to fix it anyhow, even if you could. . . ."

"Don't you want me to do nothing for you then anymore?" He turned with a slight movement toward her, his eyes falling on her breasts.

"I can't stand the pressure, I can't," she shouted back at him. "Why did you have to go and do it?"

"I didn't do nothing," he explained, as though trying to remember what had been said and what had not. "That's why it's so odd. They just felt I looked like I was going to, and they fired me."

"Jesus, I don't understand," she said, but without any tears on her face now. "Why did this have to happen to me when I can't bear to hear about anything that ain't human."

But her husband was not listening to her words or noticing whether she had tears or not. He was looking only at what was she, this fat, slightly middle-aged woman. She looked as though she had come to her permanent age, and he knew then that though he was but twenty-eight, he might as well be sixty, and the something awful and permanent that comes to everybody had come at last to him. Everything had come to an end, whether because he had looked at boys, or whether because the men had suddenly decided that yes, there was something odd in his character.

"Peaches," he said, and as he paused in his speech, the name he had always called her seemed to move over into the silence and vacancy of the broken refrigerator. "I will always stand by you anyhow, Peaches Maud."

You Reach for Your Hat

PEOPLE saw her every night on the main street. She went out just as it was getting dark, when the street lights would pop on, one by one, and the first bats would fly out round Mrs. Bilderbach's. That was Jennie. Now what was she up to? everyone would ask, and we all knew, in company and out. Jennie Esmond was off for her evening walk and to renew old acquaintances. Now don't go into details, the housewives would say over the telephone. Ain't life dreary enough without knowing? They all knew anyhow as in a movie they had seen five times and where the sad part makes them cry just as much the last showing as the first.

They couldn't say too much, though. Didn't she have the gold star in the window, meaning Lafe was dead in the service of his country? They couldn't say too much, and, after all, what did Jennie do when she went out? There wasn't any proof she went the whole hog. She only went to the Mecca, which had been a saloon in old World War days and where no ladies went. And, after all, she simply drank a few beers and joked with the boys. Yes, and well, once they told that she played the piano there, but it was some sort of old-fashioned number and everybody clapped politely after she stopped.

She bought all her clothes at a store run by a young Syrian. Nobody liked him or his merchandise, but he did sell cheap and he had the kind of things that went with her hair, that dead-straw color people in town called angel hair. She bought all her dresses there that last fall and summer, and they said the bargain she got them for no one would ever believe.

61

Then a scandalous thing. She took the gold star out of the window. What could it mean? Nobody had ever dreamed of such a thing. You would have thought anyone on such shaky ground would have left it up forever. And she took it down six months after the sad news. It must mean marriage. The little foreign man. But the janitor said nobody ever called on her except Mamie Jordan and little Blake Higgins.

She went right on with her evening promenades, window-shopping the little there was to window-shop, nodding to folks in parked cars and to old married friends going in and out of the drug store. It wasn't right for a woman like Jennie to be always walking up and down the main street night after night and acting, really acting, as if she had no home to go to. She took on in her way as bad as the loafers had in front of the court house before the mayor ordered the benches carried away so they couldn't sit down. Once somebody saw her in the section around the brewery and we wondered. Of course, everyone supposed the government paid her for Lafe's death; so it wasn't as if she was destitute.

Nobody ever heard her mention Lafe, but Mamie Jordan said she had a picture of him in civilian clothes in her bedroom. He wasn't even smiling. Mamie said Jennie had had such trouble getting him to go to Mr. Hart's photography studio. It was right before his induction, and Jennie had harped on it so long that Lafe finally went, but he was so mad all the time they were taking him he never smiled once; they had to finish him just looking. Mamie said Jennie never showed any interest in the picture and even had toilet articles in front of it. No crepe on it or anything.

Mamie didn't understand it at all. Right after he was reported missing in action she went down to offer her sympathy and Jennie was sitting there eating chocolates. She had come to have a good cry with her and there she was cool as a cucumber. You'd never have known a thing had happened. It made Mamie feel so bad, because she had always liked Lafe even if he never would set the world on fire, and she had burst out crying, and then after a little while Jennie cried too and they sat there together all evening weeping and hugging each other.

But even then Jennie didn't say anything about Lafe's going really meaning anything to her. It was as though he had been gone for twenty years. An old hurt. Mamie got to thinking about it and going a little deeper into such a mystery. It came back to her that Lafe had always gone to the Mecca tavern and left Jennie at home, and now here she was out there every night of her life.

Mamie thought these things over on her way to the movie that night. No one had ever mentioned Jennie's case lately to her, and, truth to tell, people were beginning to forget who Lafe was. People don't remember anymore. When she was a girl they had remembered a dead man a little longer, but today men came and went too fast; somebody went somewhere every week, and how could you keep fresh in your memory such a big list of departed ones?

She sighed. She had hoped she would run into Jennie on her way to the movie. She walked around the court house and past the newspaper office and she went out of her way to go by the drygoods store in hopes she would see her, but not a sign. It was double feature night; so she knew she would never get out in time to see Jennie after the show.

But the movie excited her more than ever, and she came out feeling too nervous to go home. She walked down the main street straight north, and before she knew it she was in front of the Mecca. Some laboring men were out front and she felt absolutely humiliated. She didn't know what on earth had come over her. She looked in the window and as she did so she half expected the men to make some under-handed move or say something low-down, but they hardly looked at her. She put her hands to the glass, pressing her nose flat and peering in so that she could see clear to the back of the room.

She saw Jennie all right, alone, at one of the last tables. Almost before she knew what she was doing, she was walking through the front door. She felt herself blushing the most terrible red ever, going into a saloon where there were no tables for ladies and before dozens of coarse laboring men, who were probably laughing at her.

Jennie looked up at her, but she didn't seem surprised.

"Sit down, Mamie." She acted just as cool as if they were at her apartment.

"I walked past," Mamie explained, still standing. "I couldn't help noticing you from outside."

"Sweet of you to come in," Jennie went on. Something in the dogged, weary quality of her voice gave Mamie her chance. She brought it right out: "Jennie, is it because you miss him so that you're . . . here?"

The old friend looked up quickly. "Dear Mame," she said, laughing, "that's the first time I've heard you mention him in I don't know how long."

Jennie simply kept on looking about as if she might perhaps find an explanation for not only why she was here but for the why of anything.

"I wish you would let me help you," Mamie continued. "I don't suppose you would come home with me. I suppose it's still early for you. I know my 'Lish always said time passed so fast with beer."

Jennie kept gazing at this frowsy old widow who was in turn gazing at her even more intently. She looked like her dead mother the way she stared.

"I understand," Mamie repeated. She was always saying something like that, but Jennie didn't weigh her friend's words very carefully. She wasn't quite sure just who Mamie was or what her friendship stood for, but she somehow accepted them both tonight and brought them close to her.

"You may as well drink. May as well be sheared for a sheep as a lamb."

"I believe I will," Mamie said, a kind of belligerence coming into her faded voice.

"Charley," Jennie called, "give Mamie some bottle beer."

The "girls" sat there laughing over it all.

The smile began to fade from Jennie's mouth. She looked at her old friend again as if trying to keep fresh in her mind that she was really sitting there, that she had come especially.

Mamie had that waiting look on her face that old women always have.

The younger woman pulled the tiny creased photograph from her purse. Mamie took it avidly. Yes, it was coming, she knew. At last Jennie was going to pour herself out to her. She would know everything. At last nothing would be held back. In her excitement at the thought of the revelation to come, she took several swallows of beer. "Tell me," she kept saying. "You can tell old Mamie."

"He wasn't such a bad looker," Jennie said.

The friend leaned forward eagerly. "Lafe?" she said. "Why, Lafe was handsome, honey. Didn't you know that? He was." And she held the picture farther forward and shook her head sorrowfully but admiringly.

"If he had shaved off that little mustache, he would have been better looking. I was always after him to shave it off, but somehow he wouldn't. Well, you know, his mouth was crooked . . . ."

"Oh, don't say those things," Mamie scolded. "Not about the dead." But she immediately slapped her hand against her own mouth, closing out the last word. Oh, she hadn't meant to bring that word out! We don't use that word about loved ones.

Jennie laughed a little, the laugh an older woman might have used in correcting a small girl.

"I always wondered if it hurt him much when he died," she said. "He never was a real lively one, but he had a kind of hard, enduring quality in him that must have been hard to put out. He must have died slow and hard and knowing to the end."

Mamie didn't know exactly where to take up the thread from there. She hadn't planned for this drift in the conversation. She wanted to have a sweet memory talk and she would have liked to reach for Jennie's hand to comfort her, but she couldn't do it now the talk had taken this drift. She took another long swallow of beer. It was nasty, but it calmed one a little.

"I look at his picture every night before I climb in bed,"

Jennie went on. "I don't know why I do. I never loved him, you know."

"Now, Jennie, dear," she began, but her protest was scarcely heard in the big room. She had meant to come forward boldly with the "You did love him, dear," but something gray and awful entered the world for her. At that moment she didn't quite believe even in the kind of love which she had seen depicted that very night in the movies and which, she knew, was the only kind that filled the bill.

"You never loved him!" Mamie repeated the words and they echoed dully. It was a statement which did not bear repeating; she realized that as soon as it was out of her mouth.

But Jennie went right on. "No, I never did love Lafe Esmond."

"Closing time!" Charley called out.

Mamie looked around apprehensively.

"That don't apply to us," Jennie explained. "Charley lets me stay many a night until four."

It was that call of closing time that took her back to her days at the cigar factory when fellows would wait in their cars for her after work. She got to thinking of Scott Jeffreys in his new Studebaker.

She looked down at her hands to see if they were still as lovely as he had said. She couldn't tell in the dim light, and besides, well, yes, why not say it, who cared about her hands now? Who cared about any part of her now?

"My hands were lovely once," Jennie said aloud. "My mother told me they were nearly every night and it was true. Nearly every night she would come into my bedroom and say, 'Those lovely white hands should never have to work. My little girl was meant for better things.'"

Mamie swallowed the last of the bottle and nodded her head for Jennie to go on.

"But do you think Lafe ever looked at my hands? He never looked at anybody's hands. He wasn't actually interested in woman's charm. No man really is. It only suggests the other to them, the thing they want out of us and always get. They only start off by complimenting us on our figures. Lafe wasn't interested in anything I had, And I did have a lot once. My mother knew I was beautiful."

She stopped. This was all so different from anything Mamie had come for. Yes, she had come for such a different story.

"Lafe married me because he was lonesome. That's all. If it hadn't been me it would have been some other fool. Men want a place to put up. They get the roam taken out of them and they want to light. I never loved him or anything he did to me. I only pretended when we were together.

"I was never really fond of any man from the first."

Mamie pressed her finger tightly on the glass as if begging a silent power in some way to stop her.

"I was in love with a boy in the eighth grade and that was the only time. What they call puppy love. Douglas Fleetwood was only a child. I always thought of forests and shepherds when I heard his name. He had beautiful chestnut hair. He left his shirt open winter and summer and he had brown eyes like a calf's. I never hardly spoke to him all the time I went to school. He was crippled, too, poor thing, and I could have caught up with him any day on the way home, he went so slow, but I was content to just lag behind him and watch him. I can still see his crutches moving under his arms."

Mamie was beginning to weep a little, a kind of weeping that will come from disappointment and confusion, the slow heavy controlled weeping women will give when they see their ideals go down.

"He died," Jennie said.

"When Miss Matthias announced it in home economics class that awful January day, I threw up my arms and made a kind of whistling sound, and she must have thought I was sick because she said 'Jennie, you may be excused.'

"Then there were those nice boys at the cigar factory, like I told you, but it never got to be the real thing, and then Lafe came on the scene."

Here Jennie stopped suddenly and laughed rather loudly. Charley, who was at the other end of the room, took this for some friendly comment on the lateness of the hour and waved and laughed in return.

Mamie was stealthily helping herself to some beer from Jennie's bottle.

"Drink it, Mame," she said. "I bought it for you, you old toper." Mamie wiped a tear away from her left eye.

"As I said, I was tired of the cigar factory and there was Lafe every Friday at the Green Mill dance hall. We got married after the big Thanksgiving ball."

"Why, I think I remember that," Mamie brightened. "Didn't I know you then?"

But Jennie's only answer was to pour her friend another glass.

"He went to the foundry every morning after I had got up to cook his breakfast. He wouldn't go to the restaurants like other men. I always had such an ugly kimono to get breakfast in. I was a fright. He could at least have given me a good-looking wrapper to do that morning work in. Then there I was in the house from 4:30 in the A.M. till night waiting for him to come back. I thought I'd die. I was so worn out waiting for him I couldn't be civil when he come in. I was always frying chops when he come."

She took a big drink of beer.

"Everything smelled of chops in that house. He had to have them."

Charley began again calling closing time. He said everybody had to clear the place.

"It ain't four o'clock, is it?" Mamie inquired.

"No, not yet. I don't know what come over Charley tonight. He seems to want to get rid of us early. It's only one-thirty. I suppose some good-lookin' woman is waiting for him."

Yes, the Mecca was closing. Jennie thought, then, of the places she had read about in the Sunday papers, places where pleasure joints never closed, always open night and day, where you could sit right through one evening into another, drinking and forgetting, or remembering. She heard there were places like that in New Orleans where they had this life, but mixed up with colored people and foreigners. Not classy at all and nothing a girl would want to keep in her book of memories.

And here she was all alone, unless, of course, you could count Mamie.

"I was attractive once," she went on doggedly. "Men turned around every time I went to Cincinnati."

Mamie, however, was no longer listening attentively. The story had somehow got beyond her as certain movies of a sophisticated slant sometimes did with her. She was not sure at this stage what Jennie's beauty or her lack of it had to do with her life, and her life was not at all clear to her. It seemed to her in her fumy state that Jennie had had to cook entirely too many chops for her husband and that she had needed a wrapper, but beyond that she could recall only the blasphemies against love.

"My mother would have never dreamed I would come to this lonely period. My mother always said that a good-looking woman is never lonely. 'Jennie,' she used to say, 'keep your good looks if you don't do another thing.'"

The craven inattention, however, of Mamie Jordan demanded notice. Jennie considered her case for a moment. Yes, there could be no doubt about it. Mamie was hopelessly, unbelievably drunk. And she was far from sober herself.

"Mamie Jordan," she said severely, "are you going to be all right?"

The old friend looked up. Was it the accusation of drink or the tone of cruelty in the voice that made her suddenly burst into tears? She did not know, but she sat there now weeping, loudly and disconsolately.

"Don't keep it up any more, Jennie," she said. "You've said such awful things tonight, honey. Don't do it anymore. Leave me my little mental comforts."

Jennie stared uncomprehendingly. The sobs of the old woman vaguely filled the great empty hall of the drinking men.

It was the crying, she knew, of an old woman who wanted something that was fine, something that didn't exist. It was the crying for the idea of love like in songs and books, the love that wasn't there. She wanted to comfort her. She wanted to take her in her arms and tell her everything would be all right. But she couldn't think of anything really convincing to say on that score. She looked around anxiously as if to find the answer written on a wall, but all her eyes finally came to rest on was a puddle of spilled beer with Lafe Esmond's picture swimming in the middle.

No, you can't really feel sorry for yourself when you see yourself in another, and Jennie had had what Mamie was having now too many times, the sorrow with drink as the sick day dawned.

But the peculiar sadness evinced by Mamie's tears would not go away. The sore spot deep in the folds of the flesh refused to be deadened this time, and it was this physical pang which brought her back to Lafe. She saw him as if for a few illumined seconds almost as though she had never seen him before, as though he were existing for her for the first time. She didn't see exactly how the dead could know or Lafe could be in any other world looking down on her, and yet she felt just then that some understanding had been made at last between them.

But it was soon over, the feeling of his existing at all. Lafe wasn't coming back and nobody else was coming back to her either. If she had loved him she would have had some kind of happiness in looking at his photograph and crying like Mamie wanted her to. There would be consolation in that. Or even if they had brought him home to her so she would be able to visit the grave and go through the show and motions of grief. But what was him was already scattered so far and wide they could never go fetch any part of it back.

Clasping Mamie by the arm, then, and unfolding the handkerchief to give to her, she had the feeling that she had been to see a movie all over again and that for the second time she had wept right in the same place. There isn't anything to say about such private sorrow. You just wait till the lights go on and then reach for your hat.

A Good Woman

MAUD did not find life in Martinsville very interesting, it is true, but it was Mamie who was always telling her that there were brighter spots elsewhere. She did not believe Mamie and said so.

Mamie had lived in St. Louis when her husband was an official at the head of a pipeline company there. Then he had lost his job and Mamie had come to Martinsville to live. She regretted everything and especially her marriage, but then she had gradually resigned herself to being a small town woman.

Mamie was so different from Maud. "Maud, you are happy," she would say. "You are the small town type, I guess. You don't seem to be craving the things I crave. I want something and you don't."

"What is it you want?" Maud asked.

The two women were sitting in Hannah's drug store having a strawberry soda. Mamie was reminded, she said, of some old-fashioned beer parties she and her husband had been invited to in Milwaukee when they were younger.

Mamie did not know what it was she wanted. She felt something catch at her heart strings on these cool June days and she would purposely remind herself that summer would soon be over. She always felt the passing of summer most keenly before it had actually begun. Fall affected her in a strange way and she would almost weep when she saw the falling maple leaves or the blackbirds gathering in flocks in deserted baseball parks.

"Maud, I am not young," Mamie would say, thinking of

71

how bald and whitish and grubby her husband was getting.

Maud put down her ice-cream spoon, the straw hanging half out of the dish, and looked at her. Maud was every bit three years younger than Mamie, but when her best friend talked the way she did, Maud would take out her purse mirror and stare wonderingly through the flecks of powder on the glass. Maud had never been beautiful and she was getting stout. More and more she was spending a great deal of money on cosmetics that Mr. Hannah's young clerk told her were imported from a French town on the sea coast.

"If I could only leave off the sweets," Maud said, finishing her soda.

"Maud, are you happy?" Mamie sighed. But Maud did not answer. She had never particularly thought about happiness; it was Mamie who was always reminding her of that word. Maud had always lived in Martinsville and had never thought much about what made people happy or unhappy. When her mother died, she had felt lonely because they had always been companions. For they were not so much like mother and daughter as like two young women past their first youth who knew what life was. They had spent together many a happy afternoon saying and doing foolish young things, in the summer walking in the parks and fairgrounds and in the winter making preserves and roasting fowl for Thanksgiving and Christmas parties. She always remembered her mother with pleasure instead of grief. But now she had Mamie for a friend and she was married to Obie.

Her marriage to Obie had been her greatest experience, but she did not think about it much any more. Sometimes she almost wished Obie would go away so that she could remember more clearly the first time she had met him when he was an orchestra leader in a little traveling jazz band that made one-night stands near the airport in Martinsville. Obie had been so good looking in those days, and he was still pretty much the same Obie, of course, but he was not Obie the bandleader anymore. But once he had quit playing in orchestras and had become a traveling salesman, Maud's real romance had ended and she could only look out her window on to the muddy Ohio River and dream away an afternoon.

Obie and Mamie had talks about Maud sometimes. "We spend too much," Obie would say to her. He said he lived on practically nothing on the road. They both agreed she was not very practical. And she spent too much on cosmetics and movies. Mamie did not say so much about the movies because she knew she was the cause there of Maud's spending more than her income allowed, but then it was not Mamie surely who advised her the night of the carnival to buy that imported ostrich plume fan with the ruby jewels in the center and a good many other things of the same kind. And how could Maud give up the pleasure of the movies, or the ice-cream or perfumes she got at Mr. Hannah's drug store? And what would Mr. Hannah do for star customers, for that was what Mamie said she and Maud were. They were actually out of all Martinsville his star customers, though they never purchased anything in his pharmacal department.

"Maud," Mamie said, "what do we get out of life anyway?"

Maud was not pleased with Mamie's taking this turn in the conversation. She did not like to get serious in the drug store as it spoiled her enjoyment of the ice cream and she had to think up an answer quickly on account of Mamie's impatience or Mamie would not be pleased and would think she was slow-witted, and she was sure Mamie thought she was slow-witted anyhow.

When Maud left Mamie that day she began to think it over. She walked slowly down the street, going north away from Mr. Hannah's drug store.

Mr. Hannah was standing by his green-trimmed display window, watching her as she walked to her yellow frame house over the river.

"What do we get out of life anyway?" Mamie's words kept humming about in her mind but she was so tired from the exhaustion of the warm dusty day that she did not let herself think too much about it. She did not see why Mamie had to keep thinking of such unpleasant things. It depressed her a little, too, and she did not like the feeling of depression. She did not want to think of sad things or whether life was worth living. She knew that Mamie always enjoyed the sad movies with unhappy endings, but she could never bear them at all. Life is too full of that sort of thing, she always told Mamie, and Mamie would say, pouting and giving her a disappointed look, "Maud, you are like all small town housewives. You don't know what I am feeling. You don't feel things down in you the way I feel them."

As she sauntered along she saw Bruce Hauser in front of his bicycle shop. Bruce was a youngish man always covered with oil and grease from repairing motorcycles and machines. When he smiled at Maud she could see that even his smile was stained with oil and car paint and she found herself admiring his white teeth.

She heard some school boys and girls laughing and riding over the bridge on their bicycles and she knew that school was out for the summer and that was why they were riding around like they were. It had not been so very long since she had gone to school, she thought, and for the second time that day she remembered her mother and the warm afternoons when she would come home from school and throw her books down on the sofa and take down her red hair, and her mother and she would eat a ripe fruit together, or sometimes they would make gooseberry preserves or marmalade. It was all very near and very distant.

The next day she felt a little easier at finding Mamie in a better humor and they went to a movie at the Bijou. It was a comedy this afternoon and Maud laughed quite a lot. On the way home Mamie complained that the movie had done nothing to her, had left her, she said, like an icicle, and she felt like asking for her money back.

When they sat down in Hannah's drug store, they began reading the BILL OF FARE WITH SPECIALTIES — for though they had sat in the same booth for nearly five years and knew all the dishes and drinks, they still went on reading the menu as if they did not know exactly what might be served. Suddenly Mamie said, "Are you getting along all right with Obie, Maud?"

Maud raised her too heavily penciled eyebrows and thought over Mamie's question, but instead of letting her answer, Mamie went on talking about the movie, and when they were leaving the drug store, Maud told Mr. Hannah to charge her soda.

"Why don't you let me pay for yours?" Mamie said, pulling her dress which had stuck to her skin from the sticky heat of the day.

Maud knew that Mamie would never pay for her soda even if she happened to be flat broke and hungry. She knew Mamie was tight, but she liked her anyway. Maud owed quite a bill at Mr. Hannah's and nearly all of it was for strawberry sodas. If Obie had known it, Maud would have been in trouble all right, but she always managed to keep Obie from knowing.

"I know," Mamie said on the way home, "I know, honey, that you and Obie don't hit it off right any more."

Maud wondered how Mamie knew that, but what could she say to deny it? She said, "Obie has to work out of town too much to be the family man I would like him to be."

When Maud got home that night she found that Obie had arrived. He was a little cross because she had not prepared dinner for him.

"I was not sure you was coming," Maud said.

She prepared his favorite dinner of fried pork chops and French fried potatoes with a beet and lettuce salad and some coffee with canned milk and homemade preserves and cake.

"Where was you all day?" Obie asked at the table, and Maud told him she usually went to a movie with Mamie Sucher and afterwards she went to the drug store and got a soda.

"You ought to cut down on the sweets," Obie said, and Maud remembered having caught a reflection of herself that day in the hall mirror, and she knew she was a long way from having the same figure she had had as a girl. For a moment she felt almost depressed as Mamie said she was all the time.

While Maud was doing the dishes, Obie told her that he had some good news for her, but she knew from the first it was not really good news. Obie told her that he had quit his traveling job and was going to sell life insurance now. He said he was getting too old to be on the road all the time. He wanted to have a little home life for a change, and it wasn't right for Maud to be alone so much.

Maud did not know what to say to him. The tears were falling over her hands into the dishwater, for she knew Obie would never make as much money selling life insurance as he had made on the road as a traveling salesman, and she knew there wouldn't be any more money for her for a long while. And all of a sudden she thought of the time when she had first begun getting stout and the high school boys had quit asking her for dances at the Rainbow Gardens and didn't notice her anymore.

The next time Maud saw Mamie was a week later, and Mamie was curious to know everything and asked how Obie was getting along these days.

"He quit his sales work," Maud said, and she felt the tears beginning to come, but she held them back by breathing deeper.

"I'm not a bit surprised," Mamie said. "I saw it coming all the time."

They walked over to the movie, and it was a very sad one. It was about a woman who had led, as Maud could see, not a very virtuous life. She had talked with three or four such women in her lifetime. The woman in the picture gave up the man she was in love with and went away to a bigger town. Mamie enjoyed it very much.

On the way home Mamie wanted Maud to come and have a soda.

"A strawberry soda?" Maud said, putting on some more lipstick and looking in at the green display windows with their headache ads and pictures of cornplasters. "I can't afford it."

"What do you mean, you can't afford it?" Mamie said.

"Obie has to make good at his insurance first," Maud told her.

"Come on in and I will buy you one," Mamie said in a

hard firm voice, and though Maud knew Mamie did not want to spend money on her, she couldn't bear to go home to an empty house without first having some refreshment, so she went in with her.

As soon as they had finished having their sodas, Mr. Hannah came over to Maud and said he would like to have a few words in private with her.

"I am paying for this," Mamie said as if she suspected trouble of some sort.

Maud made a motion with her hand and started to walk with Mr. Hannah toward the pharmacy room.

"Do you want me to wait outside?" Mamie said, but she got no reply.

An old woman with white gloves was sitting in a booth looking at Maud and Mr. Hannah. Maud knew her story and kept looking at her. She was to have married a young business man from Baltimore, but the day before the wedding the young man had died in a railroad accident. Ever since then, the old woman had not taken off her white wedding gloves.

"Well, Maud," said Mr. Hannah, his gray old eyes narrowing under his spectacles, "I've been meaning to talk over with you the little matter of your bill and have been wondering whether or not . . ."

Maud could feel the red coming up over her face. She knew the old woman with the white gloves was hearing all of it. Maud feared perhaps she had put on too much rouge, for Mr. Hannah was giving her peculiar looks.

"How much is the bill?" she managed to say.

Mr. Hannah looked over his books, but he did not need to look to know how much Maud owed.

"Thirty-five dollars," he said.

Maud moved slightly backwards. "Thirty-five?" she repeated without believing, and she looked over on the books where her account was listed in black purplish ink. "Surely," Maud said, "that must be a mistake."

"Well, you have been having sodas on credit for more than six months," Mr. Hannah said, grinning a little.

"Not surely thirty-five dollars' worth," Maud told him, working the clasp on her purse, "because," she said, "I can't pay it, Obie isn't making full salary and I can't give it to you now at all."

"No hurry to collect yet," Mr. Hannah said and there was a little warmth coming into his voice. "Ain't no hurry for that," he said.

Suddenly Maud could not control her tears. They were falling through her fingers into a small handkerchief embroidered with a blue bird and a rose bush.

"No, Maud," Mr. Hannah said, "I will be real easy on you. Maybe you would like to talk it all over in the pharmacy room," he said taking her arm, and before she knew her own mind he had led her into the back room.

"Don't in any case," Maud begged him, sobbing a little, "don't in any case, Mr. Hannah, tell my husband about this bill."

"No need at all, no need at all," he said, turning on the light in the pharmacy room. Mr. Hannah was staring at her. Maud was not beautiful, really. Her powder-spotted mirror told her that, and she had a receding chin and large pores. But Mr. Hannah was looking. She remembered now how he had led a singing class at the First Presbyterian Church and he had directed some girls to sing "America the Beautiful" in such a revised improper way that the elders had asked him to leave the church, and he had, and soon after that his wife had divorced him.

As Mamie Sucher was not there to prompt her, Maud did not know what more to say to him. She stood there looking at the bill. She knew it could not be thirty-five dollars. She knew she was being cheated and yet she could not tell him to his face he was lying. It was the only drug store in town where she could get sodas on credit. All the other stores made you pay on leaving or before you drank your soda. Maud stood there paralyzed, looking at the bill, and her face felt hot and sticky.

Then Mr. Hannah said something that pleased her. She

did not know why it pleased her so much. "Maud, you beautiful girl, you," he said.

He was holding her hand, the hand with her mother's ruby ring. "Why don't you ever come into the pharmacy room," he said. "Why do you have to wait for an invitation, good friends like us?" And he clasped her hand so tightly that the ring pressed against her index finger, painfully. She had never been in the pharmacy room before but she did not like the whiffs of drugs and the smell of old cartons of patent medicines that came from there. "Maud, you beauty," he said.

Maud knew that she should say something cold and polite to Mr. Hannah, but suddenly she could not. She smiled and as she smiled the rouge cracked a little on her lips. Mr. Hannah was saying, "Maud, you know you don't have to stand on form with an old friend of the family like me. You know, Maud, I knowed you when you was only a small girl. I knowed your mother well, too."

She laughed again and then she listened to the flies on the screen, the flies that were collecting there and would be let in.

She tried to take the bill from his hand. "I will give it to my husband," she said.

"He will be very mad," Mr. Hannah warned her.

"Yes," Maud breathed hard. It wasn't possible for a man like Obie to believe that she could come into this drug store of Mr. Hannah's and buy only strawberry sodas and make that large a bill, and she knew Obie would never believe her if she told him.

"Well, give me the bill, Mr. Hannah," she said, but Mr. Hannah was still muttering about how dangerous such little things were to the happiness of young married people. Maud thought right then of a time when her mother had gone walking with her and Maud had a new pink parasol and all of a sudden a dirty alley cur had jumped on her as if to spoil her new parasol, not purposely but only in play, and she had said, "Oh, hell," and to hear her swear for the first time had given her mother a good laugh. And now she said so that

Mr. Hannah could scarcely hear, "Oh, hell," and he laughed suddenly and put his arm around her.

She had thought everything like that was over for her and here was Mr. Hannah hugging her and calling her "beauty."

She knew it was not proper for her to be in this position with an old man like Mr. Hannah, but he wasn't doing anything really bad and he was so old anyhow, so she let him hug her and kiss her a few times and then she pushed him away.

"I ain't in no hurry to collect, you know that, Maud," Mr. Hannah said, and he had lost his breath and was standing there before her, his old faded eyes watering.

"Of course, my husband ought to see this bill," Maud said, but she just couldn't make the words have any force to sound like she meant it.

"You just go home and forget about it for a while, why don't you, Maud," he said.

She kept pushing a black imitation cameo bracelet back and forth on her arm. "You know how my husband would feel against it," she said.

Then Mr. Hannah did something that was even more surprising. He suddenly tore up the bill right in front of her.

Maud let out a little cry and then Mr. Hannah moved closer to her and Maud said, "No, Mr. Hannah, no, you let me make this right with you because Obie will soon be getting a check." She became actually frightened then with him in the dark, stale-smelling pharmacy room. "Some day," she said, "some day I will make this right," and she hurried out away from Mr. Hannah and she walked quickly, almost unconsciously, to the screen door where the flies were collecting before a summer thunder shower.

"I will make this right," she said, and the old druggist followed her and shouted after her, "You don't need to tell him, Maud."

"Don't call me Maud," she gasped.

She stopped and looked at him standing there. She laughed. The screen door slammed behind her and she was in the street.

It was getting a little late and Mamie was gone and the street was almost empty. She felt so excited that she would have liked to talk to Mamie and tell her what had happened to her, but she was too excited to talk to anyone and she hurried straight toward her house near the river.

Just as she got to the bridge she saw Bruce Hauser. She said, "Good evening, Bruce, how are you?" She could not say any more, she was that excited, and without waiting a minute to talk to Bruce, she took out her key and unlocked the door. As she was about to go up the stairs, she caught a reflection of herself in the hall mirror. She stared into it. Maud felt so much pleasure seeing herself so young, that she repeated Mr. Hannah's words again, "Maud, you beauty, you beauty." She was as pretty and carefree this June day as she had been that time when she and her mother had walked with the new pink parasol — long before she had met Obie — and they had joked together, not like mother and daughter, but like two good girl chums away at school.

Plan Now to Attend

FRED PARKER had not seen Mr. Graitop since college days and yet he recognized him at once. Mr. Graitop's face had not changed in twenty years, his doll-small mouth was still the same size, his hair was as immaculately groomed as a department store dummy. Mr. Graitop had always in fact resembled a department store dummy, his face wax-like, his eyes innocent and vacant, the doll-like mouth bloodless and expressionless, the body loose and yet heavy as though the passions and anguish of man had never coursed through it.

Fred on the other hand felt old and used, and he was almost unwilling to make himself known to Mr. Graitop. The fact that he remembered him as Mr. Graitop instead of by his first name was also significant. One did not really believe that Mr. Graitop had a first name, though he did and it was Ezra. Fred had remembered him all these years as Mister. And now here he was like a statue in a museum, looking very young still and at the same time ancient, as though he had never been new.

"Mr. Graitop!" Fred cried in the lobby of the hotel. The hotel was said to be one of the world's largest, perhaps the largest, and Fred felt somehow the significance of his meeting the great man here where they were both so dwarfed by physical immensity, their voices lost in the vastness of the lobby whose roof seemed to lose itself in space indefinitely.

Mr. Graitop's face broke into a faint but actual smile and his eyes shone as though a candle had been lighted behind his brain.

"You are *him*," Fred said with relief. He was afraid that

perhaps there was another man in the world who looked like Graitop.

"Yes, you are not deceived in me," Mr. Graitop said, pale and serious.

Fred was going to say *twenty years,* but he decided this was not necessary. He was not sure that Graitop would know it was twenty years, for he had always denied facts of any kind, changing a fact immediately into a spiritual symbol. For instance, in the old days if Fred had said, "It has been twenty minutes," Graitop would have said, "Well, *some* time has passed, of course." He would have denied the twenty because they were figures.

"You are just the same, Mr. Graitop," Fred said, and almost at once he wished he had not called to him, that he had hurried out of the world's largest hotel without ever knowing whether this was the real Graitop or only his twenty-year younger double.

As they were at the entrance of the Magnolia Bar, Fred ventured to ask him if he would have a drink, although it was only ten o'clock in the morning.

Mr. Graitop hesitated. Perhaps because he did remember it was twenty years, however, he nodded a quiet assent, but his face had again emphasized the bloodless doll expression, and one felt the presence of his small rat-terrier teeth pressed against the dead mouth.

"Mr. Graitop, this is unbelievable. Really not credible."

Mr. Graitop made odd little noises in his mouth and nose like a small boy who is being praised and admonished by the teacher at the same time.

Fred Parker already felt drunk from the excitement of having made such a terrible mistake as to renew acquaintance with a man who had been great as a youth and was now such a very great man he was known in the movement as the great man.

"What is your drink now, Mr. Graitop?" Fred spoke as though on a telephone across the continent . . . . "After twenty years," he explained, awkwardly laughing.

Mr. Graitop winced, and Fred felt that he did so because

he did not like to be called by his last name even though he
would not have liked to be called by his first, and perhaps
also he did not like the twenty years referred to.

As Graitop did not answer immediately but continued to
make the small-boy sounds in his nose and throat, Fred
asked in a loud voice, "Bourbon and water, perhaps?"

"Bourbon and water," Mr. Graitop repeated wearily, but
at the same time with a somewhat relieved note to his voice
as though he had recognized his duty and now with great
fatigue was about to perform it.

"I can't tell you how odd this is," Fred said nervously em-
phatic when they had been served.

"Yes, you said that before," Mr. Graitop said and his face
was as immobile as cloth.

"But it is, you know. I think it's odd that I recognized
you."

"You do?" Mr. Graitop sipped the drink as though he felt
some chemical change already taking place in his mouth and
facial muscles and perhaps fearful his changeless expression
would move.

Then there was silence and strangely enough Mr. Graitop
broke it by saying, "Your name is Fred, isn't it."

"Yes," Fred replied, paralyzed with emotion, and with
his drink untouched. He suddenly noticed that Graitop had
finished his.

"Graitop, won't you have another?" Fred asked, no invitation in his voice.

Graitop stared at him as though he had not understood
actually that he had already finished one.

"Don't you drink, sir?" Fred said, surprised at once to hear
his own question.

"No," Graitop replied.

"Another bourbon and water," Fred told the bartender.

"You know," Fred began, "this reminds me of one se-
mester when we were roommates and we neither of us went
to the football game. We could hear the crowd roaring from
our room. It sounded like some kind of mammoth animal

that was being punished. It was too hot for football and you tried to convert me to atheism."

Mr. Graitop did not say anything. Everybody had heard of his great success in introducing "new Religion" to America so that when many people thought of "new Religion" they thought immediately of Graitop.

It was a surprise to Fred to remember that Graitop had been a practicing atheist in the college quadrangles, for he remembered it only this instant.

"You were one, you know," Fred said almost viciously.

"We are always moving toward the one path," Graitop said dreamily, drinking his second drink.

Although Fred was a hard drinker, he had swiftly lost all his appetite for it, and he knew that it was not the early hour. Very often at this hour, setting out as a salesman, he was completely oiled.

"Is it the new religion that keeps you looking so kind of embalmed and youthful," Fred said, as though he had had his usual five brandies.

"Fred," Mr. Graitop said on his third drink, with mechanical composure, "it is the only conceivable path."

"I liked you better as an infidel," Fred said. "You looked more human then, too, and older. I suppose you go to all the football games now that you're a famous man."

"I suppose I see a good many," Graitop said.

"Fred," Mr. Graitop said, closing his eyes softly, and as he did so he looked remarkably older, "why can't you come with us this time?"

Fred did not know what to say because he did not exactly understand the question.

"There is no real reason to refuse. You are a living embodiment of what we all are without *the* prop."

"I'm not following you now," Fred replied.

"You are, but you won't let yourself," Graitop said, opening his eyes and finishing his third drink. He tapped the glass as though it had been an offering for Fred.

Fred signaled for another drink for Graitop just as in the past he would have for himself. His own first drink remained untouched, which he could not understand, except he felt nauseated. He realized also that he hated the great man and had always hated him.

"Well, what am I?" Fred said as he watched Graitop start on his fourth drink.

"The embodiment of the crooked stick that would be made straight," the great man replied.

"You really do go for that, don't you. That is," Fred continued, "you have made that talk part of your life."

"There is no talk involved," Mr. Graitop said. "No talk, Fred."

I wonder why the old bastard is drinking so much, Fred nearly spoke aloud. Then: "Graitop, nobody has ever understood what makes you tick."

"That is unimportant," his friend replied. "It, too, is talk."

"Nobody ever even really liked you, though I don't suppose anybody ever liked St. Paul either."

"Of course, Fred, you are really with us in spirit," Graitop said as though he had not heard the last statement.

Fred looked at his drink which seemed cavernous as a well.

"Graitop," he said stonily, "you discovered Jesus late. Later than me. I'd had all that when I was twelve . . . ."

"You're part of the new movement and your denying it here to me only confirms it," Mr. Graitop informed him.

"I don't want to be part of it," Fred began and he tasted some of his drink, but Graitop immediately interrupted.

"It isn't important that you don't want to be part: you are part and there is nothing you can do about it. You're with us."

"I couldn't be with you," Fred began, feeling coming up within him a fierce anger, and he hardly knew at what it was directed, for it seemed to be larger than just his dislike, suspicion, and dread of Graitop.

Then Mr. Graitop must have realized what only the bartender had sensed from the beginning, that he was not only drunk but going to be sick. Fred had not noticed it at all, for he felt that he had suddenly been seized and forced to relive the impotence and stupidity of his adolescence.

With the bartender's help, he assisted Mr. Graitop out of the bar. In the elevator, Graitop grew loud and belligerent and shouted several times: "It's the only path, the only way."

"What is your room number?" Fred said hollow-voiced as they got out of the elevator.

"You are really part of our group," Graitop replied.

Fred took the key out of Graitop's pocket and nodded to the woman at the desk who stared at them.

"You are completely oiled," Fred informed Graitop when the latter had lain down on the bed. "And yet it doesn't convince me any more than your preaching."

"I wonder if I had appointments," Graitop said weakly. "I was to speak to some of our people . . . ."

"I wonder which of us feels more terrible," Fred replied. "This meeting after twenty years [and he shouted the number] has been poison to both of us. We hate one another and everything we stand for. At least I hate you. You are probably too big a fraud to admit hate. I'm saying this cold sober, too, although I guess just the inside of a bar oils me up."

"You are a living embodiment of sin and sorrow and yet you are dear to us," Graitop said, looking at the ceiling.

"What the hell are you the living embodiment of, what?" Fred said and he began loosening his friend's clothing. Before he knew it, he had completely undressed Mr. Graitop as mechanically as he undressed himself when drunk. As his friend lay there, a man of at least forty, Fred was amazed to see that he looked like a boy of sixteen. Almost nothing had touched him in the world. So amazed and objective was Fred's surprise that he took the bed lamp and held it to his face and body to see if he was not deceived and this forty-year-old man was not actually a palimpsest of slightly hidden decay and senility. But the light revealed nothing but what his eye had first seen — a youth untouched by life and disappointment.

He looked so much like God or something mythological

that before he knew what he was doing Fred Parker had kissed him dutifully on the forehead.

"Why did you do that?" Mr. Graitop said, touching the place with his finger, and his voice was almost human.

Fred Parker sat down in a large easy chair and loosened his necktie. He did not answer the question because he had not heard it. He felt intoxicated and seriously unwell.

"How in hell do you live, Graitop?" he said almost too softly to be heard. "Are you married and do you have kids?"

"Yes, yes," Graitop replied, and he began to drivel now from his mouth.

Fred got up and wiped off his lips, and put the covers over him.

"A missionary," Fred Parker said. "But of what?"

"Don't be a fool," Graitop said sleepily. Suddenly he was asleep.

Fred Parker watched him again angrily from the chair.

"Who in hell are you, Graitop?" he shouted from the chair. "Why in hell did I run into you. Why in hell did I speak to you . . . . Why don't you look and act like other men?"

Fred called room service for ice, whiskey, and water. He began immediately the serious drinking he should not have been without all morning.

"When the bastard is conscious, I will ask him who he is and what he means to do."

"It's all right, Fred," Mr. Graitop said from time to time from the bed. "You are really with us, and it's all all right."

"I wish you wouldn't use that goddamn language, Graitop," he said. "You don't have the personality for a missionary. Too young and dead looking. Too vague."

From the bed there came sounds like a small boy sleeping.

Sound of Talking

In the morning Mrs. Farebrother would put her husband in the wheelchair and talk to him while she made breakfast. As breakfast time came to an end he would sink his thumb into the black cherry preserves or sometimes he would take out an old Roman coin he had picked up from the war in Italy and hold that tight. In the summertime it helped to watch the swallows flying around when the pain was intense in his legs, or to listen to a plane going quite far off, and then hear all sound stop. There was a relief from the sound then that made you almost think your own pain had quit.

This morning began when Mrs. Farebrother thought of her trip to the city the day before, how she stared at the two young men on the train, for they reminded her of two brothers she had known in high school, and of course her visit to the bird store.

As her husband's pain grew more acute, which happened every morning after breakfast, she would talk faster, which she knew irritated him more, but she felt that it distracted him more from his pain than anything else. Her voice was a different kind of pain to him, and that was diversion. For a while he held on to an iron bar when he had suffered, then he had pressed the Roman coin, and now he dabbed in the cherry preserves like a child.

"You know what I would like?" Mrs. Farebrother said. "I almost bought one yesterday in the bird store."

She moved his wheelchair closer to the window before telling him. "A raven."

"Well," he grunted, not letting his pain or anger speak

this early. He hated birds, even the swallows which he watched from the kitchen were not silent enough for him.

"Ever since I was a little girl those birds have fascinated me. I never realized until the other day that I wanted one. I was walking down the intersection and I heard the birds' voices being broadcast from that huge seed store, all kinds of birds broadcasting to that busy street. I thought a bird might be a kind of an amusement to us."

Here Mrs. Farebrother stopped talking as she moved him again, her eyes trying to avoid looking at his legs. Many times she did not know where to look, she knew he did not like her to look at him at all, but she had to look somewhere, and their kitchen was small and what one saw of the outdoors was limited.

"Do you need your pill," she said with too great a swiftness.

"I don't want it," he answered.

"I have plenty of nice ice water this morning," she said, which was a lie. She didn't know why she lied to him all the time. Her anguish and indecision put the lies into her mouth like the priest giving her the wafer on Sunday.

"Tell me about the bird store," he said, and she knew he must be in unusual pain and she felt she had brought it on him by telling about her outing. Yet if she had made him begin to suffer, she must finish what had started him on it, she could not let him sit in his wheelchair and not hear more.

"I went up two flights to where they keep the birds," she began, trying to keep her eyes away from his body and not to watch how his throat distended, with the arteries pounding like an athlete's, his upper body looking more muscular and powerful each day under the punishment that came from lower down. But his suffering was too terrible and too familiar for her to scrutinize, and in fact she hardly ever looked at him carefully: all her glances were sideways, furtive; she had found the word in the cross-word puzzles one evening *clandestine;* it was a word which she had never said to anybody and it described her and haunted her like a face you can't quite remember the name for which keeps popping up in your mind. When they lay together in bed she touched him in a clandestine way also as though she might damage him; she felt his injuries were somehow more sensitive to her touch than they were to the hand of the doctor. She slept very poorly, but the doctor insisted that she sleep with him. As she lay in the bed with him, she thought of only two things, one that he could not approach her and the other when would he die.

Thinking like this, she had forgotten she was telling a story about the bird store. It was his contemptuous stare that brought her back to her own talking: "It was a menagerie of birds," she said, and stopped again.

"Go on," he said as though impatient for what could not possibly interest him.

"Vergil," she said looking at his face. "Verge."

She did not want to tell the story about the raven because she knew how infuriating it was to him to hear about pets of any kind. He hated all pets, he had killed their cat by throwing it out from the wheelchair against a tree. And all day long he sat and killed flies with a swiftness that had great fury in it.

"The men up there were so polite and attentive," she said, hardly stopping to remember whether they were or not, and thinking again of the young men on the bus. "I was surprised because in cities you know how people are, brusque, never expecting to see you again. I hadn't gone up there to see anything more than a few old yellow canaries when what on earth do you suppose I saw but this raven. I have never seen anything like it in my life, and even the man in the shop saw how surprised and interested I was in the bird. What on earth is that? I said, and just then it talked back to me. It said, *George is dead, George is dead*."

"George is *what?*" Vergil cried at her, and for a moment she looked at him straight in the face. He looked as though the pain had left him, there was so much surprise in his expression.

"George is dead," she said and suddenly by the stillness of the room she felt the weight of the words which she had not realized until then. Sometimes, as now, when the pain left his face all her desire came back for him, while at night when she lay next to him nothing drew her to him at all; his dead weight seeming scarcely human. She thought briefly again about the hospital for paraplegics the doctor had told her about, in California, but she could never have mentioned even *paraplegic* to Vergil, let alone the place.

"What was the guy in the bird shop like?" he said, as though to help her to her next speech.

"Oh, an old guy sixty or seventy," Mrs. Farebrother lied. "He said he had clipped the bird's tongue himself. He started to describe how he did it, but I couldn't bear to hear him. Anything that involves cutting or surgery," she tried to stop but as though she had to, she added, "Even a bird . . . ."

"For Christ's sake," Vergil said.

"I have never seen such purple in wings," Mrs. Farebrother went on, as though a needle had skipped a passage on the record and she was far ahead in her speech. "The only other time I ever saw such a color was in the hair of a young Roumanian fellow I went to high school with. When the light was just right, his hair had that purple sheen. Why, in fact, they called him the raven; isn't that odd, I had forgotten . . . ."

"Let's not start your when-I-was-young talk."

She thought that when he grunted out words like this or when he merely grunted in pain he sounded like somebody going to the toilet, and even though it was tragic she sometimes almost laughed in his face at such moments. Then again when sometimes he was suffering the most so that his hair would be damp with sweat, she felt a desire to hit him across the face, and these unexplained feelings frightened her a great deal.

But today she did not want him to suffer, and that is why she did not like to tell about the raven; she knew it was hurting him somehow — why she did not know, it was nothing, it bored her as she told it, and yet he insisted on hearing everything. She knew that if he kept insisting on more details she would invent some; often that happened. He would keep asking about the things that went on outside and she would invent little facts to amuse him. Yet these "facts" did not seem to please him, and life described outside, whether true or false, tortured him.

"Oh, Verge, I wished for you," she said, knowing immediately what she had said was the wrong thing to say; yet everything was somehow wrong to say to him.

"Then I said to the man in charge, doesn't the raven ever say anything but George is . . . ." She stopped, choking with laughter; she had a laugh which Vergil had once told her sounded fake, but which somehow she could not find in her to change even for him.

"Then the man gave me a little speech about ravens," Mrs. Farebrother said.

"Well?" he said impatiently. His insistence on details had made her tired and gradually she was forgetting what things had happened and what things had not, what things and words could be said to him, what not. Everything in the end bore the warning FORBIDDEN.

"He said you have to teach the birds yourself. He said they have made no effort to teach them to talk." Mrs. Farebrother stopped trying to remember what the man had said, and what he had looked like.

"Well, he must have taught the bird to say *George is dead*," Vergil observed, watching her closely.

"Yes, I suppose he did teach him that," she agreed, laughing shrilly.

"Had there been somebody there named George?" he said, curious.

"I'm sure I don't know," she said abstractedly. She began dusting an old picture-frame made of shells. "I imagine the bird just heard someone say that somewhere, maybe in the place where they got it from."

"Where did they get it from?" he wondered.

"I'm sure nobody knows," she replied, and she began to hum.

"*George is dead*," he repeated. "I don't believe it said that."

"Why, Verge," she replied, her dust rag suddenly catching in the ruined shells of the frame. Tired as her mind was and many as the lies were she had told, to the best of her knowledge the bird had said that. She had not even thought it too odd until she had repeated it.

"Maybe the old man's name was George," Mrs. Farebrother said, not very convincing. A whole whirlwind of words waited for her again: "I asked him the price then, and do you know how much he wanted for that old bird, well not old, perhaps, I guess it was young for a raven, they live forever . . . . Fifty dollars!" she sighed. "Fifty dollars without the cage!"

He watched her closely and then to her surprise he drew a wallet out from his dressing gown. She had not known he kept a wallet there, and though his hands shook terribly, he insisted on opening it himself. He took out five ten-dollar bills, which oddly enough was all that was in it, and handed them to her.

"Why, Verge, that isn't necessary, dear," she said, and she put her hands to her hair in a ridiculous gesture.

"Don't talk with that crying voice, for Christ's sake," he said. "You sound like my old woman."

"Darling," she tried to control her tears, "I don't need any pet like that around the house. Besides, it would make you nervous."

"Do you want him or don't you," he said furiously, pushing up his chest and throat to get the words out.

She stopped in front of the wheelchair, trying to think what she *did* want: nearly everything had become irrelevant or even too obscure to bear thinking about. She fingered the five ten-dollar bills, trying to find an answer to please both of them. Then suddenly she knew she wanted nothing. She did not believe anybody could give her anything. One thing or another or nothing were all the same.

"Don't you want your raven," he continued in his firm strong male voice, the voice he always used after an attack had passed so that he seemed to resemble somebody she had known in another place and time.

"I don't really want it, Vergil," Mrs. Farebrother said quietly, handing him the bills.

He must have noticed the absence of self-pity or any attempt to act a part, which in the past had been her stock-in-trade. There was nothing but the emptiness of the truth on her face: she wanted nothing.

"I'll tell you what, Verge," she began again with her laugh and the lies beginning at the same time, as she watched him put the money back in his wallet. Her voice had become soothing and low, the voice she used on children she sometimes stopped on the street to engage in conversation. "I'm afraid of that bird, Vergil," she confessed, as though the secret were out. "It's so large and its beak and claws rather frightened me. Even that old man was cautious with it."

"Yet you had all this stuff about ravens and Roumanians and high school," he accused her.

"Oh, high school," she said, and her mouth filled with saliva, as though it was only her mouth now, which, lying to him continually, had the seat of her emotions.

"It might cheer things up for you if something talked for you around here," he said.

She looked at him to determine the meaning of his words, but she could find no expression in them or in him.

"It would be trouble," she said. "Birds are dirty."

"But if *you* want him, Verge," and in her voice and eyes there was the supplication for hope, as if she had said, If somebody would tell her a thing to hope for maybe she would want something again, have desire again.

"No," he replied, turning the wheel of the chair swiftly, "I don't want a raven for myself if you are that cool about getting it."

He looked down at the wallet, and then his gaze fell swiftly to the legs that lay on the wheelchair's footrest. She had mentioned high school as the place where life had stopped for her; he remembered further back even than Italy, back to the first time he had ever gone to the barbershop, his small legs had then hung down helplessly too while he got his first haircut; but they had hung *alive*.

"Of course you could teach the bird to talk," she said, using her fake laugh.

"Yes, I enjoy hearing talk so much," and he laughed now almost like her.

She turned to look at him. She wanted to scream or push him roughly, she wanted to tell him to just *want* something, anything for just one moment so that she could want something for that one moment too. She wanted him to want something so that she could want something, but she knew he would never want at all again. There would be suffering, the suffering that would make him swell in the chair until he looked like a god in ecstasy, but it would all be just a man practicing for death, and the suffering illusion. And why should a man practicing for death take time out to teach a bird to talk?

"There doesn't seem to be any ice after all," Mrs. Farebrother said, pretending to look in the icebox. It was time for his medicine, and she had quit looking at anything, and their long day together had begun.

Cutting Edge

MRS. ZELLER opposed her son's beard. She was in her house in Florida when she saw him wearing it for the first time. It was as though her mind had come to a full stop. This large full-bearded man entered the room and she remembered always later how ugly he had looked and how frightened she felt seeing him in the house; then the realization it was someone she knew, and finally the terror of recognition.

He had kissed her, which he didn't often do, and she recognized in this his attempt to make her discomfort the more painful. He held the beard to her face for a long time, then he released her as though she had suddenly disgusted him.

"Why did you do it?" she asked. She was, he saw, almost broken by the recognition.

"I didn't dare tell you and come."

"That's of course true," Mrs. Zeller said. "It would have been worse. You'll have to shave it off, of course. Nobody must see you. Your father of course didn't have the courage to warn me, but I knew something was wrong the minute he entered the house ahead of you. I suppose he's upstairs laughing now. But it's not a laughing matter."

Mrs. Zeller's anger turned against her absent husband as though all error began and ended with him. "I suppose he likes it." Her dislike of Mr. Zeller struck her son as staggeringly great at that moment.

He looked at his mother and was surprised to see how young she was. She did not look much older than he did. Perhaps she looked younger now that he had his beard.

"I had no idea a son of mine would do such a thing," she said. "But why a beard, for heaven's sake," she cried, as though he had chosen something permanent and irreparable which would destroy all that they were.

"Is it because you are an artist? No, don't answer me," she commanded. "I can't stand to hear any explanation from you . . . ."

"I have always wanted to wear a beard," her son said. "I remember wanting one as a child."

"I don't remember that at all," Mrs. Zeller said.

"I remember it quite well. I was in the summer house near that old broken-down wall and I told Ellen Whitelaw I wanted to have a beard when I grew up."

"Ellen Whitelaw, that big fat stupid thing. I haven't thought of her in years."

Mrs. Zeller was almost as much agitated by the memory of Ellen Whitelaw as by her son's beard.

"You didn't like Ellen Whitelaw," her son told her, trying to remember how they had acted when they were together.

"She was a common and inefficient servant," Mrs. Zeller said, more quietly now, masking her feelings from her son.

"I suppose *he* liked her," the son pretended surprise, the cool cynical tone coming into his voice.

"Oh, your father," Mrs. Zeller said.

"Did he then?" the son asked.

"Didn't he like all of them?" she asked. The beard had changed this much already between them, she talked to him now about his father's character, while the old man stayed up in the bedroom fearing a scene.

"Didn't he always," she repeated, as though appealing to this new hirsute man.

"So," the son said, accepting what he already knew.

"Ellen Whitelaw, for God's sake," Mrs. Zeller said. The name of the servant girl brought back many other faces and rooms which she did not know were in her memory. These faces and rooms served to make the bearded man who stared

at her less and less the boy she remembered in the days of
Ellen Whitelaw.

"You must shave it off," Mrs. Zeller said.

"What makes you think I would do that?" the boy wondered.

"You heard me. Do you want to drive me out of my
mind?"

"But I'm not going to. Or rather it's not going to."

"I will appeal to him, though a lot of good it will do,"
Mrs. Zeller said. "He ought to do something once in twenty
years at least."

"You mean," the son said laughing, "he hasn't done anything in that long."

"Nothing I can really remember," Mrs. Zeller told him.

"It will be interesting to hear you appeal to him," the boy
said. "I haven't heard you do that in such a long time."

"I don't think you ever heard me."

"I did, though," he told her. "It was in the days of Ellen
Whitelaw again, in fact."

"In *those* days," Mrs. Zeller wondered. "I don't see how
that could be."

"Well, it was. I can remember that much."

"You couldn't have been more than four years old. How
could you remember then?"

"I heard you say to him, *You have to ask her to go.*"

Mrs. Zeller did not say anything. She really could not remember the words, but she supposed that the scene was true
and that he actually remembered.

"Please shave off that terrible beard. If you only knew how
awful it looks on you. You can't see anything else but it."

"Everyone in New York thought it was particularly fine."

"Particularly fine," she paused over his phrase as though
its meaning eluded her.

"It's nauseating," she was firm again in her judgment.

"I'm not going to do away with it," he said, just as firm.

She did not recognize his firmness, but she saw everything
changing a little, including perhaps the old man upstairs.

"Are you going to appeal' to him?" The son laughed again when he saw she could say no more.

"Don't mock me," the mother said. "I will speak to your father." She pretended decorum. "You can't go anywhere with us, you know."

He looked unmoved.

"I don't want any of my friends to see you. You'll have to stay in the house or go to your own places. You can't go out with us to our places and see our friends. I hope none of the neighbors see you. If they ask who you are, I won't tell them."

"I'll tell them then."

They were not angry, they talked it out like that, while the old man was upstairs.

"Do you suppose he is drinking or asleep?" she said finally.

*   *

"I thought he looked good in it, Fern," Mr. Zeller said.

"What about it makes him look good?" she said.

"It fills out his face," Mr. Zeller said, looking at the wallpaper and surprised he had never noticed what a pattern it had before; it showed the sacrifice of some sort of animal by a youth.

He almost asked his wife how she had come to pick out this pattern, but her growing fury checked him.

He saw her mouth and throat moving with unspoken words.

"Where is he now?" Mr. Zeller wondered.

"What does that matter where he is?" she said. "He has to be somewhere while he's home, but he can't go out with us."

"How idiotic," Mr. Zeller said, and he looked at his wife straight in the face for a second.

"Why did you say that?" She tried to quiet herself down.

"The way you go on about nothing, Fern." For a moment a kind of revolt announced itself in his manner, but then his eyes went back to the wallpaper, and she resumed her tone of victor.

"I've told him he must either cut it off or go back to New York."

"Why is it a beard upsets you so?" he wondered, almost to himself.

"It's not the beard so much. It's the way he is now too. And it disfigures him so. I don't recognize him at all now when he wears it."

"So, he's never done anything of his own before," Mr. Zeller protested suddenly.

"Never done anything!" He could feel her anger covering him and glancing off like hot sun onto the wallpaper.

"That's right," he repeated. "He's never done anything. I say let him keep the beard and I'm not going to talk to him about it." His gaze lifted toward her but rested finally only on her hands and skirt.

"This is still my house," she said, "and I have to live in this town."

"When they had the centennial in Collins, everybody wore beards."

"I have to live in this town," she repeated.

"I won't talk to him about it," Mr. Zeller said.

It was as though the voice of Ellen Whitelaw reached her saying, *So that was how you appealed to him.*

✦   ✦

She sat on the deck chair on the porch and smoked five cigarettes. The two men were somewhere in the house and she had the feeling now that she only roomed here. She wished more than that the beard was gone that her son had never mentioned Ellen Whitelaw. She found herself thinking only about her. Then she thought that now twenty years later she could not have afforded a servant, not even her.

She supposed the girl was dead. She did not know why, but she was sure she was.

She thought also that she should have mentioned her name to Mr. Zeller. It might have broken him down about the beard, but she supposed not. He had been just as adamant and unfeeling with her about the girl as he was now about her son.

Her son came though the house in front of her without speaking, dressed only in his shorts and, when he had got safely beyond her in the garden, he took off those so that he was completely naked with his back to her, and lay down in the sun.

She held the cigarette in her hand until it began to burn her finger. She felt she should not move from the place where she was and yet she did not know where to go inside the house and she did not know what pretext to use for going inside.

In the brilliant sun his body, already tanned, matched his shining black beard.

She wanted to appeal to her husband again and she knew then she could never again. She wanted to call a friend and tell her but she had no friend to whom she could tell this.

The events of the day, like a curtain of extreme bulk, cut her off from her son and husband. She had always ruled the house and them even during the awful Ellen Whitelaw days and now as though they did not even recognize her, they had taken over. She was not even here. Her son could walk naked with a beard in front of her as though she did not exist. She had nothing to fight them with, nothing to make them see with. They ignored her as Mr. Zeller had when he looked at the wallpaper and refused to discuss their son.

*   *

"You can grow it back when you're in New York," Mr. Zeller told his son.

He did not say anything about his son lying naked before him in the garden but he felt insulted almost as much as his mother had, yet he needed his son's permission and consent now and perhaps that was why he did not mention the insult of his nakedness.

"I don't know why I have to act like a little boy all the time with you both."

"If you were here alone with me you could do anything you wanted. You know I never asked anything of you . . . ."

When his son did not answer, Mr. Zeller said, "Did I?"

"That was the trouble," the son said.

"What?" the father wondered.

"You never wanted anything from me and you never wanted to give me anything. I didn't matter to you."

"Well, I'm sorry," the father said doggedly.

"Those were the days of Ellen Whitelaw," the son said in tones like the mother.

"For God's sake," the father said and he put a piece of grass between his teeth.

He was a man who kept everything down inside of him, everything had been tied and fastened so long there was no part of him any more that could struggle against the stricture of his life.

There were no words between them for some time; then Mr. Zeller could hear himself bringing the question out: "Did she mention that girl?"

"Who?" The son pretended blankness.

"Our servant."

The son wanted to pretend again blankness but it was too much work. He answered: "No, I mentioned it. To her surprise."

"Don't you see how it is?" the father went on to the present. "She doesn't speak to either of us now and if you're still wearing the beard when you leave it's me she will be punishing six months from now."

"And you want me to save you from your wife."

"Bobby," the father said, using the childhood tone and inflection. "I wish you would put some clothes on too when you're in the garden. With me it doesn't matter, you could do anything. I never asked you anything. But with her . . . ."

"God damn *her*," the boy said.

The father could not protest. He pleaded with his eyes at his son.

The son looked at his father and he could see suddenly also the youth hidden in his father's face. He was young like his mother. They were both young people who had learned nothing from life, were stopped and drifting where they were twenty years before with Ellen Whitelaw. Only *she,* the son thought, must have learned from life, must have gone on to some development in her character, while they had been tied to the shore where she had left them.

"Imagine living with someone for six months and not speaking," the father said as if to himself. "That happened once before, you know, when you were a little boy."

"I don't remember that," the son said, some concession in his voice.

"You were only four," the father told him.

"I believe this is the only thing I ever asked of you," the father said. "Isn't that odd, I can't remember ever asking you anything else. Can you?"

The son looked coldly away at the sky and then answered, contempt and pity struggling together, "No, I can't."

"Thank you, Bobby," the father said.

"Only don't *plead* any more, for Christ's sake." The son turned from him.

"You've only two more days with us, and if you shaved it off and put on just a few clothes, it would help me through the year with her."

He spoke as though it would be his last year.

"Why don't you beat some sense into her?" The son turned to him again.

The father's gaze fell for the first time complete on his son's nakedness.

✦   ✦

Bobby had said he would be painting in the storeroom and she could send up a sandwich from time to time, and Mr. and Mrs. Zeller were left downstairs together. She refused to allow her husband to answer the phone.

In the evening Bobby came down dressed carefully and his beard combed immaculately and looking, they both thought, curled.

They talked about things like horse racing, in which they were all somehow passionately interested, but which they now discussed irritably as though it too were a menace to their lives. They talked about the uselessness of art and why people went into it with a detachment that would have made an outsider think that Bobby was as unconnected with it as a jockey or oil magnate. They condemned nearly everything and then the son went upstairs and they saw one another again briefly at bedtime.

The night before he was to leave they heard him up all hours, the water running, and the dropping of things made of metal.

Both parents were afraid to get up and ask him if he was all right. He was like a wealthy relative who had commanded them never to question him or interfere with his movements even if he was dying.

He was waiting for them at breakfast, dressed only in his shorts but he looked more naked than he ever had in the garden because his beard was gone. Over his chin lay savage and profound scratches as though he had removed the hair with a hunting knife and pincers.

Mrs. Zeller held her breast and turned to the coffee and Mr. Zeller said only his son's name and sat down with last night's newspaper.

"What time does your plane go?" Mrs. Zeller said in a dead, muffled voice.

The son began putting a white paste on the scratches of his face and did not answer.

"I believe your mother asked you a question," Mr. Zeller said, pale and shaking.

"Ten-forty," the son replied.

The son and the mother exchanged glances and he could see at once that his sacrifice had been in vain: she would also see the beard there again under the scratches and the gashes he had inflicted on himself, and he would never really be her son again. Even for his father it must be much the same. He had come home as a stranger who despised them and he had shown his nakedness to both of them. All three longed for separation and release.

But Bobby could not control the anger coming up in him, and his rage took an old form. He poured the coffee into his saucer because Mr. Zeller's mother had always done this and it had infuriated Mrs. Zeller because of its low-class implications.

He drank viciously from the saucer, blowing loudly.

Both parents watched him helplessly like insects suddenly swept against the screen.

"It's not too long till Christmas," Mr. Zeller brought out. "We hope you'll come back for the whole vacation."

"We do," Mrs. Zeller said in a voice completely unlike her own.

"So," Bobby began, but the torrent of anger would not let him say the thousand fierce things he had ready.

Instead, he blew savagely from the saucer and spilled some onto the chaste white summer rug below him. Mrs. Zeller did not move.

"I would invite you to New York," Bobby said quietly now, "but of course I will have the beard there and it wouldn't work for you."

"Yes," Mr. Zeller said, incoherent.

"I do hope you don't think I've been . . . ." Mrs. Zeller cried suddenly, and they both waited to hear whether she was going to weep or not, but she stopped herself perhaps by the realization that she had no tears and that the feelings which had come over her about Bobby were likewise spent.

"I can't think of any more I can do for you," Bobby said suddenly.

They both stared at each other as though he had actually left and they were alone at last.

"Is there anything more you want me to do?" he said, coldly vicious.

They did not answer.

"I hate and despise what both of you have done to yourselves, but the thought that you would be sitting here in your middle-class crap not speaking to one another is too much even for me. That's why I did it, I guess, and not out of any love. I didn't want you to think that."

He sloshed in the saucer.

"Bobby," Mr. Zeller said.

The son brought out his *What?* with such finished beauty of coolness that he paused to admire his own control and mastery.

"Please, Bobby," Mr. Zeller said.

They could all three of them hear a thousand speeches. The agony of awkwardness was made unendurable by the iciness of the son, and all three paused over this glacial control which had come to him out of art and New York, as though it was the fruit of their lives and the culmination of their twenty years.

63: Dream Palace

63 : *Dream Palace*

"Do you ever think about Fenton Riddleway?" Parkhearst Cratty asked the greatwoman one afternoon when they were sitting in the summer garden of her "mansion."

Although the greatwoman had been drinking earlier in the day, she was almost sober at the time Parkhearst put this question to her.

It was a rhetorical and idle question, but Parkhearst's idle questions were always put to her as a plea that they should review their lives together, and she always accepted the plea by saying nearly the same thing: "Why don't you write down what Fenton did?" she would say. "Since you did write once," and her face much more than her voice darkened at him.

Actually the eyes of the greatwoman were blackened very little with mascara and yet such was their cavernous appearance they gaped at Parkhearst as though tonight they would yield him her real identity and why people called her great.

"Fenton Riddleway is vague as a dream to me," the greatwoman said.

"That means he is more real to you than anybody," Parkhearst said.

"How could it mean anything else?" she repeated her own eternal rejoinder. Then arranging her long dress so that it covered the floor before her shoes, she began to throw her head back as though suffering from a feeling of suffocation.

It was her signal to him that he was to leave, but he took no notice of her wishes today.

113

"I can't write down what Fenton did because I never found out who he was," Parkhearst explained again to her.

"You've said that ever since he was first with us. And since he went away, a million times."

She reached for the gin; it was the only drink she would have since the days of Fenton.

"Not that I'm criticizing you for saying it," she said. "How could *I* criticize you?" she added.

"Then don't scratch and tear at me, for Christ's sake," he told her.

Her mouth wet from the drink smiled faintly at him.

"What Fenton did was almost the only story I ever really wanted to write," Parkhearst said, and a shadow of old happiness came over his thin brown face.

Grainger's eyes brightened briefly, then went back into their unrelieved darkness.

"You can't feel as empty of recollection as I do," Grainger mumbled, sipping again.

Parkhearst watched the veins bulge in his hands.

"Why are we dead anyhow?" Parkhearst said, bored with the necessity of returning to this daily statement. "Is it because of our losing the people we loved or because the people we found were damned?" He laughed.

One never mentioned the "real" things like this at Grainger's, and here Parkhearst had done it, and nothing happened. Instead, Grainger listened as though hearing some two or three notes of an alto sax she recalled from the concerts she gave at her home.

"This is the first time you ever said you were, Parkhearst. Dead," she said in her clearest voice.

He sat looking like a small rock that has been worked on by a swift but careless hammer.

"Are you really without a memory?" she asked, speaking now like a child.

He did not say anything and she began to get up.

"Don't get up, or you'll fall," he said, almost not looking in her direction.

The greatwoman had gotten up and stood there like some more than human personage at the end of an opera. Parkhearst closed his eyes. Then she advanced to a half-fall at the feet of her old friend.

"Are those tears?" she said looking up into his face.

"Don't be tiresome, Grainger. Go back and sit down," he said, with the petulance of a small boy.

Pushing her head towards his face, she kissed him several times.

"You're getting gray," she said, almost shocked. "I didn't know it had been such a long time."

"I try never to think about those things," he looked at her now. "Please get up."

"Do you think Fenton Riddleway would know you now, Parkhearst?" the greatwoman asked sullenly but without anything taunting in her voice.

"The real question is whether we would know Fenton Riddleway if we saw him."

"We'd know him," she said. "Above or beneath hell."

As evening came on in the "mansion" (*mansion* a word they both thought of and used all the time because Fenton had used it), they drank more and more of the neat Holland gin, but drunkenness did not take: was it after all, they kept on saying, merely the remembrance of a boy from West Virginia, that mover and shaker Fenton, that kept them talking and living.

"Tell me all about what he did again," Grainger said, seated now on her gold carved chair. The dark hid her age, so that she looked now only relatively old; it almost hid the fact that she was drunk, drunk going on to ten years, and her face was shapeless and sexless.

"Tell me what he did all over again, just this last time. If you won't write it down, Parkhearst, you'll have to come here and tell it to me once a month. I had always hoped you would write it down so I could have it to read on my bad nights . . . . "

"Your memory is so much better than mine," Parkhearst said.

"I have no memory," the greatwoman said. "Or only a grain of one."

She raised her glass threateningly, but it had got so dark in the room she could not see just where Parkhearst's tired voice was coming from. It was like the time she had called Russell long distance to his home town, the voice had wavered, then had grown, then had sunk into indistinguishable sounds. Parkhearst would take another drink of the gin, then his voice would rise a bit, only to die away again as he told her everything he could remember.

"Are you awake?" Parkhearst questioned her.

"Keep going," she said. "Don't stop to ask me a single thing. Just tell what he did, and then write it all down for me to read hereafter."

He nodded at her.

There was this park with a patriot's name near the lagoon. Parkhearst Cratty had been wandering there, not daring to go home to his wife Bella. He had done nothing in weeks, and her resentment against him would be too heavy to bear. Of course it was true, what he was later to tell Fenton himself, that he was looking for "material" for his book. Many times he had run across people in the park who had told him their stories while he pretended to listen to their voices while usually watching their persons.

In this section of the park there were no lights, and the only illumination came from the reflection of the traffic blocks away. Here the men who came to wander about as aimless and groping as he were obvious shades in hell. He always noticed this fact as he noticed there were no lights. Parkhearst paid little attention to the actual things that went on in the park and, although not a brave or strong young man, he had never felt fear in the park itself. It was its atmosphere alone that satisfied him and he remained forever innocent of its acts.

It was August, and cool, but he felt enervated as never before. His marriage pursued him like a never-ending nightmare, and he could not free himself from the obsession that "everything was over."

Just as children, he and the greatwoman Grainger longed, and especially demanded even, that something should happen, or again Parkhearst would cry, "A reward, I must have a reward. A reward for life just as I have lived it."

It was just as he had uttered the words *a reward* that he first saw Fenton Riddleway go past, he remembered.

In the darkness and the rehearsed evil of the park it was odd, indeed, as Parkhearst now reflected on the event, that anyone should have stood out at all that night, one shadow from the other. Yet Fenton was remarkable at once, perhaps for no other reason than that he was actually lost and wandering about, for no other reason than this. Parkhearst did not need to watch him for more than a moment to see his desperation.

Parkhearst lit a cigarette so that his own whereabouts would be visible to the stranger.

"Looking for anybody?" Parkhearst then asked.

Fenton's face was momentarily lighted up by Parkhearst's cigarette: the face had, he noted with accustomed uneasiness, a kind of beauty but mixed with something unsteady, unusual.

"Where do you get out?" the boy asked.

He stood directly over Parkhearst in a position a less experienced man than the writer would have taken to be a threat.

Parkhearst recognized with a certain shock that this was the first question he had ever had addressed to him in the park which was asked with the wish to be answered: somebody really wanted out of the park.

"Where do you want to go?"

Fenton took from his pocket a tiny dimestore notebook and read from the first page an address.

"It's south," Parkhearst replied. "Away from the lagoon."

Fenton still looked too unsure to speak. He dropped the notebook and when he stooped to pick it up his head twitched while his eyes looked at the writer.

"Do you want me to show you?" Parkhearst asked, pretending indifference.

Fenton looked directly into his face now.

Those eyes looked dumb, Parkhearst saw them again, like maybe the eyes of the first murderer, dumb and innocent and getting to be mad.

"Show me, please," Fenton said, and Parkhearst heard the Southern accent.

"You're from far off," Parkhearst said as they began to walk in the opposite direction of the lagoon.

Fenton had been too frightened not to want to unburden himself. He told nearly everything, as though in a police court, that he was Fenton Riddleway and that he was nineteen, that he had come with his brother Claire from West Virginia, from a town near Ronceverte, that their mother had died two weeks before, and that a friend of his named Kincaid had given him an address in a rooming house on Sixty-*three* Street . . .

"You mean Sixty-*third*," Parkhearst corrected him, but Fenton did not hear the correction then or when it was made fifty times later: "A house on Sixty-three Street," he continued. "It turns out to be a not-right-kind of place at all . . . . "

"How is that?" Parkhearst wondered.

They moved out of the middle section of the park and into a place where the street light looked down on them. Fenton was gazing at him easily but Parkhearst's eyes kept to his coat pocket, which bulged obviously.

"Is that your gun there?" he said, weary.

Fenton watched him, moving his lips quickly.

"Don't let it go off on yourself," Parkhearst said ineffectively as the boy nodded.

"But what were you saying about that house?" the writer went back to his story.

"It's alive with something, I don't know what . . . . "

Fenton's thick accent, which seemed to become thicker now, all at once irritated Parkhearst, and as they drew near the part of the city that was more inhabited and better lighted, he felt himself surprised by Fenton's incredibly poor-fitting almost filthy clothes and by the fact that his hair had the look of not ever perhaps having been cut or combed. He looked more or less like West Virginia, Parkhearst supposed, and then Parkhearst always remembered he had thought this, he looked not only just West Virginia, he looked himself, Fenton.

"What's it alive with, then?" Parkhearst came back to the subject of the house.

"I don't mean it's got ghosts, though I think it maybe does." He stopped, fishing for encouragement to go on and when none came he said: "It's a not-right house. There ain't nobody in it for one thing."

"I don't think I see," Parkhearst said, and he felt not so much his interest waning as his feeling that there was something about this boy too excessive; everything about him was too large for him, the speech, the terrible clothes, the ragged hair, the possible gun, the outlandish accent.

"All the time we're alone in it, I keep thinking how empty it is, and what are we waiting for after all, with so little money to tide us over, if he don't show up. Claire cries all the time on account of the change. The house don't do *him* any good."

"Can you find your way back now, do you think?" Parkhearst asked, as they got to a street down which ordinary people and traffic were moving.

A paralysis had struck the writer suddenly, as though all the interest he might have had in Fenton had been killed. He was beginning to be afraid also that he would be involved in more than a story.

Fenton stopped as if to remind Parkhearst that he had a responsibility toward him. His having found the first person

in his life who would listen to him had made him within
ten minutes come to regard Parkhearst as a friend, and now
the realization came quickly that this was only a listener who
having heard the story would let him go back to the "not-
right house."

"Here's fifty cents for you," Parkhearst said.

He took it with a funny quick movement as though money
for the first time had meaning for him.

"You won't come with me to see Claire?"

Parkhearst stared. This odd boy, who was probably wanted
by the police, who had come out of nothing to him, had
asked him a question in the tone of one who had known him
all his life.

"Tomorrow maybe," Parkhearst answered. He explained
lamely about Bella waiting for him and being cross if he
came any later.

The boy's face fell.

"You know where to find the house?" Fenton said, hoarse.

"Yes," Parkhearst replied dreamily, indifferent.

Fenton looked at Parkhearst, unbelieving. Then: "How
can you find it?" he wondered. "I can't ever find it no matter how many times I go and come. How can you then?"

The sorrow on Fenton's face won him over to him again,
and he felt Bella's eyes of reproach disappear from his mind
for a moment.

"Tomorrow afternoon I'll visit you at the house," he
promised. "Two o'clock."

A moment later when Fenton was gone, Parkhearst looking back could not help wait for the last sight of him in the
street, and a new feeling so close to acute sickness swept over
him. It was the wildness and freedom Fenton had, he began
to try to explain to himself. The wildness and freedom held
against his own shut-in locked life. He hurried on home to
Bella.

✶   ✶

Bella listened vaguely to the story of Fenton Riddleway.

There had been, she recalled mechanically, scores, even hundreds, of these people Parkhearst met in order to study for his writing, but the stories themselves were never put in final shape or were never written, and Parkhearst himself forgot the old models in his search for new ones.

"Is Fenton to take the place of Grainger now?" Bella commented on his enthusiasm, almost his ecstasy.

There was no criticism in her remark. She was beyond that. Bella Cratty had resigned herself to her complete knowledge of her husband's character. There was, furthermore, no opposing Parkhearst; if he were opposed he would disintegrate slowly, vanish before her eyes. He was a child who must not be crossed in the full possession of his freedom, one who must be left to follow his own whims and visions.

She had married him without anyone knowing why, but everyone agreed she had done so with the full knowledge of what he was. If she had not known before, their married life had been a continuous daily rehearsal of Parkhearst's character; he was himself every minute, taking more and more away from what was *her* with each new sorrow he brought home to her. He became more and more incurable and it was his incurable quality which made him essential to her.

She was not happy a second. Had she seen the wandering men in the park after whom Parkhearst gazed, she might have seen herself like them, wandering without purpose away from the light. And though she tried to pretend that she wanted Parkhearst to have friends no matter what they were, no matter what they would do, she never gave up suffering, and each of the "new" people he met and "studied" cost her an impossible sacrifice.

There was something at once about the name Fenton Riddleway that made her feel there was danger here in his name as Grainger was in hers. Only there was something in the new name more frightening than in Grainger's.

As two o'clock approached the following day (an evil hour in astrology, Parkhearst had noticed covertly, for Bella ob-

jected to his interest in what she called "the moons"), both
of them felt the importance of his departure. He had tried to
get her "ready" from the evening before so that she would
accept this as Fenton's day, when as a writer he must find
out all there was to know about this strange boy. Parkhearst
used the word *material* again, though he had promised himself to give up using the word.

"I suppose in the end you will let Grainger have Fenton,"
Bella remarked, a sudden hostility coming over her face as
she sat at the kitchen table drinking her coffee.

Parkhearst stopped his task of sewing on a button on his
old gray-green jacket.

It was only when his wife said that that he understood he
did not wish to share Fenton with anyone, until, he lied to
himself, he had found out every thing Fenton had done. And
then he corrected this lie in his own mind: he simply did
not want to share Fenton with anybody. Grainger would
spoil him, would take him over, if she were interested, and
he knew of course that she was going to be.

"Grainger won't get him," he said finally.

Bella laughed a very high laugh, ridden with hysteria and
shaky restraint. "You've never kept anybody from one another as long as you've been friends," she reviewed their
lives. "What would happen," she went on bitterly, "if you
couldn't show one another what you take in, what you ac-
complish. If there was no competition!"

"Fenton is different," Parkhearst said, pale with anger.
Then suddenly, so shaken by fear of what she said, he told
her a thing which he immediately realized was trivial and
silly: "He has a gun, for one thing."

Bella Cratty did not go on drinking coffee immediately,
but not due to anything Parkhearst had said except his pro-
nouncing of Fenton's name. There had, of course, in their
five years of marriage and in their five years of Grainger,
been people with guns, and people whom he had found in
streets, in parks, in holes, who had turned out to be all right,
but now she suddenly felt the last outpost of safety had been

reached. Their lives had stopped suddenly, and then were jerked ahead out of her control at last. She felt she was no longer *here*.

"Maybe Grainger *should* meet him," she said in a tone unlike herself, because there was no hysteria or pretending in it, just dull fear, and then she finished the coffee at the same moment her husband finished sewing the button on his coat.

Still holding his needle and thread, he advanced to her and kissed her on the forehead. "I know you hate all this," he said, like a doctor or soldier about to perform an heroic act. "I know you can't get used to all this. Maybe you aren't used to what is me."

Bella had not waited this time for the full effect of the kiss. She got up and quickly went into the front room and began looking out the window with the intensity of one who is about to fly out into space. He followed her there.

"Do you hate me completely?" Parkhearst asked, happy with the sense she had given him permission to go for Fenton.

It was nearly two o'clock, he noted, and she did not give him goodbye and the word to leave.

"Just go, dear," she said at last, and it was not the fact she had put on a martyr's expression in her voice, the voice was the only one that could come from her having chosen, as she had, the life five years before.

"I can't go when you sound like this," he complained. His voice told how much he wanted to go and that it was already past two o'clock.

Yet somehow the strength to give him up did not come to her. He had to find it in her for himself and take it from her.

"Go now, go," she said when he kissed the back of her neck.

"I will," he said, "because I know I'm only hurting you by staying."

Bella nodded.

When he was gone, she watched for him onto the street

below. From above she could see him waving and throwing a kiss to her as he moved on down toward Sixty-third Street. He looked younger than Christ still, she said. A boy groom . . . . Sometimes people had half-wondered, she knew, if she was his very young mother. She stood there in that stiff height so far above him and yet felt crawling somewhere far down, like a bug in a desert, hot and sticking to ground, and possibly not even any more alive.

*   *

As necessary as Bella was to his every need for existence, his only feeling of life came when he left her, as today, for a free afternoon. And this afternoon was especially free. There was even the feeling of the happiness death might give. It was only later that life was to be so like death that the idea of dying was meaningless to him, but tonight, he remembered, he had thought of death and it was full of mysterious desirability.

It was one of those heavy days in the city when a late riser is not certain it is getting light or dark, an artificial twilight in which the sounds of the elevated trains and trucks weight darkness the more. Parkhearst hurried on down the interminable street, soon leaving the white section behind, and into the beginning of the colored district. People took no notice of him, he was no stranger to these streets, and besides he was dressed in clothes which without being too poor made him inconspicuous.

He was not looking at the street anyhow today, whose meanness and filth usually gave his soul such satisfaction. His whole mind was on Fenton. Fenton was a small-town boy, and yet all his expression and gestures and being made it right that he should live on this street, where no one really belonged or stayed very long.

It was difficult, though, to see Fenton living in a house, even in the kind of house that would be near Sixty-third Street. There must be some kind of mistake there, he thought.

He went on, pursued by the memory of Fenton's face.
Was there more, he wondered out loud, in that face than
poverty and a tendency to be tricky if not criminal? What
were those eyes conveying, then, some meaning that was
truthful and honest over and above his deceit and rotten-
ness?

He was late. He hurried faster. The dark under the elevated made him confuse one street for another. He stopped
and in his indecision looked back east toward the direction
of the park where he had met Fenton: he feared Fenton had
played a trick on him, for there was nothing which resembled a house on the street. He stood in front of a fallen-in
building with the handwritten sign in chalk: THE COME
AND SEE RESURRECTION PENTECOSTAL CHURCH. REVEREND
HOSEA GULLEY, PASTOR.

Then walking on, he saw near a never-ending set of vacant
lots the house he knew must contain Fenton. It was one of
those early twentieth-century houses that have survived by
oversight but which look so rotten and devoured that you
can't believe they were ever built but that they rotted and
mushroomed into existence and that their rot was their first
and last growth.

There was no number. It was a color like green and yellow. Around the premises was a fence of sharp iron, cut like
spears.

He began knocking on the immense front door and then
waiting as though he knew there would be no answer.

As nobody stirred, he began calling out the name of his
new friend. Then he heard some faint moving around in the
back and finally Fenton, looking both black and pale, appeared through the frosted glass of the inner door and stared
out. His face greeted Parkhearst without either pleasure or
recognition, and he advanced mechanically and irritably, as
though the door had blown open and he was coming to close
it.

"No wonder you had trouble finding it," Parkhearst said
when Fenton unlocked the door and let him in.

"He's having a bad spell, that's why I'm in a hurry," Fenton explained.

"Who?" Parkhearst closed the door behind him.

"Claire, my brother Claire."

They went through a hallway as long as a half city block to a small room in which there was a dwarf-like cot with large mattress clinging to it and a crippled immense chest of drawers supported by only three legs. The window was boarded up and there was almost no light coming from a dying electric bulb hung from the high ceiling.

On the bed lay a young boy dressed in overall pants and a green sweater. He looked very pale but did not act in pain.

"He says he can't walk now," Fenton observed. "Claire, can't you say *hello* to the visitor?" Fenton went over to the bed and touched Claire on the shoulder.

"He keeps asking me why we can't move on. To a real house, I suppose," Fenton explained softly to Parkhearst. "And that worries him. There are several things that worry him," Fenton said in a bored voice.

"Look," Claire said cheerfully and with energy, pointing to the wall. There were a few bugs moving rather rapidly across the cracked calcimine. "Sit down in this chair," Fenton said and moved the chair over to Parkhearst.

"Do you really think," Fenton began on the subject that was closest to him too, "that we're *in* the right house maybe?"

Parkhearst did not speak, feeling unsure how to begin. For one thing, he was not positive that the small boy who was called Claire was not feebleminded, but the longer he looked the more he felt the boy was reasonably intelligent but probably upset by the kind of life he was leading with Fenton. He therefore did not reply to Fenton's question at once, and Fenton repeated it, almost shouting. He had gotten very much more excited since they had met in the park the evening before.

Parkhearst was noticing that Claire followed his brother with his eyes around the room with a look of both intense approval and abject dependence. It was plain that between him and nothing there was only Fenton.

"We've come to the end of our rope, I guess," Fenton said, almost forgetting that Parkhearst had not replied to his question.

"No," Parkhearst said, but Fenton hardly heard him now, talking so rapidly that his spit flew out on all sides of his mouth. He talked about their mother's funeral and how they had come to this house all because Kincaid had known them back in West Virginia and had promised them a job here. Then suddenly he picked up a book that Claire had under the bedclothes and showed it to Parkhearst as though it was both something uncommon and explanatory of their situation. The book, old and ripped, was titled *Under the Trees,* a story about logging.

"Doesn't anybody else live here?" Parkhearst inquired at last.

"We haven't heard nobody," Fenton replied. "There's so many bugs it isn't surprising everybody left, if they was here," he went on. "But Claire says there is," he looked in the direction of his brother. "Claire feels there is people here."

"I hear them all the time," Claire said.

"No, there is nobody here," Parkhearst assured both of them. "This is a vacant house and you must have made a mistake when you came in here. Or your friend Kincaid played a joke on you," he finished, seeing at once by their expression he should not have added this last sentence.

"Anyhow," Parkhearst continued awkwardly while Fenton stared at him with his strange eyes, "it's no place for you, especially with Claire sick. I think I have a plan for you, though," Parkhearst said, as though thinking through a delicate problem.

Fenton walked over very close to him as though Parkhearst were about to hand him a written paper which would explain everything and tell him and Claire what to do in regard to the entire future.

"I think Grainger will give you the help you need," he explained. He had forgotten that Fenton knew nothing about her.

Fenton turned away and looked out the boarded window. Evidently he had expected some immediate help, and Parkhearst had only spoken of a name like a matchbox, Grainger, adding later that was the last name of a wealthy woman that nobody ever called by her first name. This was discouraging because of course Fenton knew he could never do anything to please anybody with such a name.

"Grainger will like you," Parkhearst went on doggedly, knowing he was not moving Fenton at all.

"You would be interested in going to her mansion at least," he said.

Claire, following Fenton's example, showed likewise no interest in the "great woman."

"If you promise me you will go with me to the house of the 'great woman,'" Parkhearst said (using that phrase preciously and purposely just as he had mentioned Grainger without explaining who she was or that she was a woman), "I assure you we'll be able to help you between us. Really help."

He had not finished this speech when he remembered what Bella had told him about his handing over Fenton to Grainger.

Fenton turned now from the boarded window and faced him. His whole appearance had grown surprisingly ominous as though Parkhearst had destroyed some great promise and hope.

"We don't have no choice," Fenton said, his words more gentle than his expression, and he looked at Claire, although he addressed his words to no one.

"I don't know what I'll do in the house of a greatwoman," Fenton went on. "Why do you call her *great?*"

"Oh I don't know," Parkhearst replied airily. "Of course she isn't, really. But is anybody? Was anybody ever?"

"I never did hear anybody called that," Fenton said. He

looked at Claire as though he might have heard someone called that.

"Why is she great?" he wondered aloud again.

Parkhearst felt flustered despite his years of looking and collecting the "material" and talking with the most intractable of persons.

"If you come tomorrow, I feel you'll understand," Parkhearst told him, getting up. "I don't see why you act like this when you're in trouble." Then: "Where's your gun," he said irritably.

Fenton put his hand quickly to his pocket. "Fuck you," he said, feeling nothing there.

"Don't think I can get offended," Parkhearst said. "Neither your talk nor your acts. You just seemed a bit young to have any gun."

"Young?" Fenton asked, as though this had identified his age at last. His face flushed and for the first time Parkhearst noticed that there was a scar across his lip and chin.

"Please come, Fenton, when we want to help you," he said, almost as soft as some sort of prayer.

"I don't like to go in big houses. You said she was rich, too. Claire and me don't have the clothes for it . . . . Say, are you trying to make us a show for somebody?" Fenton asked, as though he had begun to understand Parkhearst. His face went no particular color as this new thought took hold of him. "Or use us? You're not trying to *use* us, are you?"

When he asked that last question, Parkhearst felt vaguely a kind of invisible knife cut through the air at him. He could not follow the sources of Fenton's knowledge. At times the boy talked dully, oafish, and again he showed complete and intuitive knowledge of the way things were and had to be.

"I want to help you," Parkhearst finally said in a womanish hurt voice.

"Why?" Fenton said in an impersonal anger. Then quickly the fight in him collapsed. He sat down on the cheap kitchen chair occupied a moment before by Parkhearst Cratty.

"All right, then, I'll come for your sake. But Claire has to stay here."

"All right, then, Fenton. I'll be here for you."

They argued a little about the hour.

Fenton did not look at Parkhearst as he said goodbye, but Claire waved to him as though seated in a moving vehicle, his head constantly turning to keep sight of the visitor.

*   *

"Who is that, Fenton?" Claire asked as soon as his brother had returned from closing the front door.

"He's a man who writes things about people," Fenton said. "He wants me to tell him things so he can write about me."

Fenton looked up at the high sick ceiling; the thought of the man writing or listening to him in order to write of him was too odd ever to be understood.

"Like you write in your little note papers?"

"No," Fenton answered, and turned to look at Claire. "I only put things down there to clear up in me what we are going to do next. Understand?"

"Why can't I see them, then, Fenton?"

"Because you can't, hear?"

"I want to read your little note papers!"

Fenton began to slap Claire, rather gently at first, and then with more force. "Don't mention it again," he said, hitting him again. "Hear?"

Claire's weeping both hurt Fenton deeply and gave him a kind of pleasure, as though in the hitting the intense burden of Claire was being lightened a little.

He had written once in the "note papers" a thought which had caused him great puzzlement. This thought was that just as he had wished Mama dead, so that he felt the agent of her death, so now he wanted Claire to be dead, and despite the fact that the only two people in the world he had loved were Mama and Claire.

Then he had to realize that the thing which stung him most about Claire when they were with strangers was his brother's not being quite right and that when he had been with the writer he had not felt this pain. There was this about the man who had turned up in the park, you did not feel any pain about telling him things, things almost as awful as those he had put down in the note papers.

"Why is it?" Fenton asked, raising his voice as though addressing a large group of people, "when I am so young I am so pissed-off feeble and low?" ,

Claire shook his head as he was accustomed to when Fenton put these questions to him. He had never answered any of them, and yet Fenton asked more and more of them when he knew that Claire did not know the answers.

Then Claire, seeing his chance, watching his brother narrowly, said, without any preparation: "I heard God again in the night."

Fenton tried to quiet himself in the tall room. It was always much easier to calm yourself outdoors or in a farmhouse, but in a small but high room like this when sorrow is heard it is hard to be quiet and calm. Fenton nevertheless made his voice cool as he said, "Claire, what did I tell you about talking like that?"

"I did." Claire began to cry a little.

"Are you going to quit talking like that or ain't you?" Fenton said, the anger welling up in him stronger than any coolness he had put into his voice.

"Don't hit me when I tell you, Fenton," Claire cried on. "Don't you want to know I hear Him?"

Fenton's hands loosened slightly. He felt cramps in his insides.

"I told you those was dreams," Fenton said.

"They ain't! I hear it all day when I don't dream . . . . "

"Maybe somebody lives here, that's all." Fenton waited as though to convince himself. "I could forgive you if you dreamed about Mama and she come running to you to say

comforting things to you. But you always talk about God.
And I strongly doubt . . . . "

"Don't say it again, Fenton, don't say it again!" Claire sat
up in bed.

" . . . not only strongly doubt but know He's not
real . . . . "

Claire let out a strange little cry when he heard the blasphemy and fell back on the bed. Claire fell so awkwardly it
made Fenton laugh.

After this, Fenton felt the cramps again and he knew he
must go out and get a drink. Yet because neither of them
had had anything to eat since morning he feared that if he
began drinking now he would not remember to get Claire
anything to eat.

He began to rub Claire's temples gently. If only they were
safe from trouble he would always be kind to Claire, but
trouble always made him mean.

"It's so crappy late out!" he began again, moving away
from Claire. "Why does it have to feel so late out everywhere?" This was one of the things which he had written
on the note papers so he wouldn't feel so burned up and
dizzy. "Even the writer says I am so young," Fenton muttered on, "yet why do I feel I only got two minutes more to
do with?"

"It's late, all right," Claire said, still weeping some, but
with a happy look on his face now. The small boy had gotten
up out of the bed and was walking over to where Fenton
now stood near the window.

"You heard me tell you to stay in bed, didn't you . . . .
Didn't you hear, crapface?"

The boy paused there in the middle of the room, his
mouth open disgustingly. But he had already turned his
mind away from Claire. He whirled out of the room and
was gone.

"He forgot his gun," Claire said looking out into the awful night of the hall. "He don't know how to use it anyhow,"
he finished and went back to the little bed.

Everything had changed so much since he had been Mama's son, nothing as little as forgetting a gun was remarkable.

"He's gone, he's gone," Claire kept repeating to himself. "Fenton's gone," he repeated on and on until he had fallen asleep again.

*   *

Fenton had soon found the taverns where his existence aroused no particular interest or comment. People occasionally noticed his accent or his haircut, but generally they ignored him. There was such an endless row of taverns and the street itself was so endless he could always choose a different tavern for each day and each drink. In the end he went to the places that served both colored and white. It would have been unreal of him to Mama had she known, but this kind of tavern made him feel the easiest, perhaps it was more like home.

He knew now (he began all over again) that Kincaid was not coming to find them in the house. And as he went on with his drink he knew that nobody was ever coming to the house because it was the "latest" time in his life and maybe the "latest" in the world.

"Then where will we end up?" he said quickly, aloud. He felt that some of the customers must have looked at him, but when he said nothing more nobody came over to him or said anything. He got out a pencil stub and wrote something on the note papers.

"Things don't go anywhere in our lives," he wrote. "Sometimes somebody like Mama dies and the whole world stops or begins to move backwards, but nothing happens to us, even her dying don't get us anywhere except maybe back. Yet you have to go on waiting, it's the one thing nobody lets up on you for. Like now we're doing for Kincaid and for what?"

Someone had left a newspaper on the bar, open to the want ad section. Fenton began reading these incomprehen-

sible notifications of jobs. Someone once had told him, perhaps Kincaid, that nobody was ever hired this way, they
were only put in there because the employers had to do it,
and actually, this somebody had told him, they were really
all hired to begin with, probably when you read about
them.

Fenton remembered again that he did not know how to
do anything. He had no skills, no knowledge. That was why'
the big old house with tall rooms was getting more ghosty
for him, it was so much like the way he was inside himself,
the house didn't work at all, and he was all stopped inside
himself too just like the house. That was why it was like a
trap, he said.

As he drank a little more he decided he must move on to
another drinking place because the bartender had begun to
watch him write in the note papers too much and it scared
him.

He went on in search of the next place, but before he
reached it he saw the ALL NIGHT THEATER, a movie house
that never closed. Instead of choosing another drinking
place, he decided to choose this, for the price of admission
was nearly the same as that of a beer.

There was the same sad smell inside, a faint stink from
old men and a few boys who had been out in the open,
standing or lying on the pavement during part of the night.
The seats did not act as though they were required to hold
you off the floor. Faces twisted around to look at you, or
somebody's hand sometimes came out of the dark and
touched you as though to determine whether you were flesh
or not.

Fenton did not notice or care about any of these things.
He scarcely looked at the picture, and half of the audience
must have been sleeping or looking at the floor, at nothing.

*   *

He did not know what time he woke up in the ALL NIGHT.

THEATER. The audience had thinned out a little. The screen showed a horse and a man crossing a desert, walking as though they were not going to go much longer if they didn't find some water or perhaps just a cool place to stop.

It was then that Fenton remembered Parkhearst Cratty and the greatwoman. For the first time he began to think about them as having some slight meaning, some relationship to himself. That is, they knew about him, and he existed for them. He had gotten as far down in the dumps as possible and still be alive, and now he began to come up a little out of where he was and to think about what Parkhearst Cratty was jawing about.

The thought that anybody called the greatwoman should want to see him struck him suddenly as so funny that he laughed out loud. Then he stopped and looked around him, but nobody was looking at him. The dead world of the shadows on the screen seemed to look at him just then more than the men around him.

Fenton sat a little while longer in the ALL NIGHT THEATER, holding his notebook down to a little of the light at the end of the aisle so that he might write down some more of what he was thinking. Then having written a little more, he gazed at the want ads again that he had carried along with him and saw the words MEN MEN MEN under the difficult light.

Finally he got hungry and walked out into the gray street. It was six o'clock in the morning and it would be a long day until night came and brought Parkhearst Cratty and his plans.

Fenton went into a cafe called CHECKER where some colored men were drinking orange pop. He ordered a cup of black coffee, and then drinking that, he ordered another. Then he ordered some rolls and ate part of those. After that he ordered some coffee and rolls to take out, and started home to Claire.

Just before getting to the house, he went back to a small tavern he had missed before and had a whiskey.

It was funny, he reflected, that before coming here to the city with its parks and vacant houses he had almost never had a drink, and now he had it, quite a bit.

Claire stared at him, his face red and swollen from bites. Fenton had him get up and they began going through the mattress looking for the bugs.

"Where was you?" Claire wanted to know.

"All Night Movie."

This answer perfectly satisfied Claire.

"Why don't you drink the coffee I brought you and eat those rolls?"

"I ain't hungry, Fenton."

"Drink the coffee like I tell you."

Fenton kept looking at the mattress. "I don't see any of the bastards," he said. "They must be inside the fucking mattress."

"Fenton," Claire soothed him. "I didn't dream last night at all or hear anything."

"So?" Fenton spoke crossly. He set the mattress down and then lazily began eating the rolls Claire had not touched.

"I didn't even feel the bugs biting," Claire said, pushing his face close to Fenton to show him, but his voice trailed off as he saw Fenton's heavy lack of interest in what he had done and thought.

Then all at once Fenton saw his brother's face, which was almost disfigured from the bites. Fenton's own fear and amazement communicated themselves frightfully to Claire.

"You look Christ awful," Fenton cried.

"Don't scare me now, Fenton," Claire began to whimper.

"I don't aim to scare you," Fenton said with growing irritability. "Have you been crying over Mama or is your face just swelled from bugs?"

"I don't know," Claire said, and he quit whimpering.

There was something terribly old and pinched now in Claire's small face.

Fenton took him by the hands and looked at his face closer.

"Ain't you well or what?" he said, the irritation coming and going in his voice, but finally yielding to a kind of sadness. "Why don't you tell me what is bothering you?" he went on.

He put his mouth on the top of Claire's head, and halfopened his lips noticing the funny little boy smell of his hair.

"You can tell me if you have been thinking about God now, if you want to, Claire."

"I ain't been thinking about Him," he said.

"Well," Fenton said, "you can if you want to. It don't matter anyhow."

"I don't think about Him," Claire said, as if from far off.

"I think I'll go to bed now," Fenton complained, looking at the cruelly narrow cot. "You slept some, didn't you, Claire."

"Yes," Claire said, a tired sad duty in his voice.

"Can I walk around outdoors now?" Claire asked, watching Fenton's oblivious brooding face.

"Yes," Fenton replied slowly. "I guess it's all right if the house is open when it's daylight. Nobody ain't coming in anyhow."

"Don't get lost, though," Fenton went on quietly as Claire began to go out.

"What's going on inside the little thing's mind?" Fenton said to himself. He loosened his heavy belt and lay down on the cot.

Fenton thought about how Claire thought about Mama. He himself thought a lot about her when actually he wasn't very aware even that he was thinking about her. Maybe he thought about her all the time and didn't even know it. But he never thought she was waiting for him on some distant star as Claire did.

"Claire," he said, beginning to sleep, "why is it one of us is even weaker than the other. When West Virginia was tough why did we come clear over here? . . . "

Even though it was day it was night really, always, in this city and night like night in caves here in the house.

Fenton lay thinking of the long time before Parkhearst Cratty would come. He thought of Parkhearst as a kind of magicman who would show different magic tricks to him, but he knew not one would take on him.

"No damn one," he said, becoming asleep.

_1   1_

It was even darker somehow when he awoke, and he knew at once that Parkhearst Cratty was there, shaking him.

"Wake up, West Virginia," Parkhearst was saying.

Fenton's mouth moved as though to let out laughter but none came, as though there were no more sound at all in him now.

"She's waiting for us," Parkhearst said.

Fenton said quiet obscene words and Parkhearst waited a little longer, situated as though nowhere in the dark.

"Where's Claire?" Parkhearst wondered vaguely.

"Ain't he here?" Fenton said.

"No," Parkhearst said, a kind of uneasiness growing in him again.

"Claire went out, but he'll be back," Fenton said, remembering.

Then when Parkhearst did not say anything in reply, Fenton said rather angrily: "I said he'd be back."

"Well, let's go, then," Parkhearst said lightly. "She gets cross when people are late," he explained.

Fenton held on to his belt as though that were what was to lift him out of bed, then got up, and turned on the light.

"You're dressed up!" He looked at Parkhearst and then down at himself.

They suddenly were both looking at Fenton's shoes, as though they couldn't help it, and as they both saw they were so miserable and ridiculous, they had to look at them objectively as horrors.

"I'm not really dressed up," Parkhearst said weakly, feeling the weakness come over him again which he always felt in Fenton's presence. "But come on, Fenton," he said, thinking of the boy's toes slightly coming through the shoes. "She's sent a taxi for us, and it's waiting."

Fenton threw a look back at the room. "So long, house," he said, and he actually waved at the room, Parkhearst noted.

They said almost nothing on the way to the greatwoman's house. Fenton kept his head down as though he were praying or sick in his stomach. He did not look out even when Parkhearst pointed out things that might have had a personal interest to him: the sight of the park where they had met, or the police station.

At last the taxi came to the house. Fenton hesitated, as though he might not get out after all. "Is this a mansion?" he asked.

Parkhearst looked at him closely. Fenton's words always had an ambiguousness about them, but there could be no ambiguousness when you studied his face: he meant just what he said, and perhaps that made the words odd.

They could hear the music from the outside.

"That is the new music the musicians are playing," Parkhearst explained. "Grainger doesn't really listen to it, but she has the musicians come because there is nothing else left to do, and it draws her circle of people to her."

Without knocking, they entered what was the most immense room Fenton had ever seen. It was almost as dark, however, as the house where he and Claire had been waiting, and the ceiling was no taller. There were a number of people sitting in corners except for one large corner of the room where some colored musicians were playing.

At the far end of the room on a slightly raised little platform, in a mammoth chair, Grainger, the greatwoman, sat, or rather hung over one side of the arm.

"My God, we're late after all," Parkhearst exclaimed. "She's too drunk to know us, I'm afraid."

Fenton began to feel a little easier once he was inside the

mansion. No one had paid him the least attention. It was, in fact, he saw with relief, not unlike the ALL NIGHT THEATER, for whatever the people were doing here in the mansion, they were paying absolutely no attention to him or Parkhearst or perhaps to anything. Yet they must have seen him, for he could see their heads move and hear their voices as they talked softly among themselves. And again like the ALL NIGHT THEATER, they were about half colored and half white.

Parkhearst was not doing anything as Fenton's attention returned slowly to him. They were in the middle of the great room, and his guide merely stood there watching Grainger. Finally, as though after a struggle with himself, he took Fenton's hand angrily and said, "Come over here, we have to go through with this."

They went up to the woman in the chair. She was possibly forty and her face was still beautiful although her mouth was slightly twisted and her throat was creased now and fat. Her eyes, although not focused on the two young men who were standing in front of her, were extremely beautiful and would have been intelligent had they not been so vacant. When Parkhearst would address her, she would immediately turn her head in the other direction.

"Grainger, I have brought Fenton Riddleway here to see you, just as you told me to do."

She did not say a word, although Parkhearst knew that she had heard him.

"She's angry," Parkhearst said, like a radio commentator assigned to a historical event which is hopelessly delayed. He sighed as though he could no longer breathe in this atmosphere.

"Everything is getting to be more difficult than anything is really worth," he pronounced.

"Please look at Fenton at least and we will leave then," he addressed Grainger.

Suddenly the greatwoman laughed and took Parkhearst's hands in her very small ones. Parkhearst gave a sound expressing relief, though his face did not lose the agonized look it had assumed the moment he recognized she was drunk.

"Are you going to be good now?" he inquired in a calmer voice.

She laughed cheerfully, like a young girl.

Fenton thought that she looked beautiful at that moment and he looked at her dress which was the kind he felt a princess in old books might have worn; it was so frighteningly white and soft and there was so much of it, it seemed to fill the little platform on which they were now all standing.

Then as Grainger's eyes moved away from Parkhearst they settled slowly and gloomily upon Fenton. They immediately expressed hostility or a kind of sullen anger. Then looking away from both of them, she picked up a drink she had placed on the floor by the chair and took a swallow so deep that she seemed to be talking to someone in the end of the glass.

"Haven't you had enough, tonight?" Parkhearst said gently. "It's that Holland stuff, too, and you promised me you wouldn't ever take that again."

"Cut that, Parkhearst, cut that," she said suddenly. "You've been boring me for a year now and I'm not listening to any more."

This was said in a tone that was tough and which was hard to connect with the soft long dress and the fine eyes.

"Well, give us something to drink then," Parkhearst retorted. "If you're sobered up enough now to be ugly, you can remember your duties as the hostess."

Grainger pointed contemptuously to a table where there were bottles and glasses. Then her gaze returned to Fenton, and the same hostility and suspicion crossed her face.

"Who is this?" she said, putting her hand on his face as one might touch what is perhaps a door in a dark house.

Fenton could only stand there, allowing her hand to be on him and looking down at her dress. He found that her gaze and touch were not unlike the soft glances that the characters on the screen of the ALL NIGHT THEATER had given him last night, looking down while he wrote what he had to write in the note papers.

His meekness and his quiet partially calmed the anger of her expression.

"Don't you like Fenton, Grainger?" Parkhearst said, returning with drinks for himself and Fenton.

"Why didn't you fill mine up too?" she said, turning bitterly to Parkhearst.

"Because you've had enough. And I'm taking the drink you now have away from you," he said, reaching for her glass.

Grainger smiled at this and put the glass into his hand.

"Now, Grainger, wake up, clear awake, and look at this boy I brought to meet you. You're always wanting to meet new people and then when I bring them to you, you get into a state like this and don't even know me when I come in. This is Fenton Riddleway."

"I saw him," the greatwoman said. She kept eyeing her drink, which Parkhearst had set on the table near her.

"How do you feel about the musicians tonight?" she inquired suddenly.

"I've heard them when they sounded more advanced," Parkhearst said. "But I wasn't listening to them at all . . . . Anyhow, the new music sounds only like its name to me now. It was only new that first night."

"So you brought Fenton to see me," she said, looking now for the first time without hostility at the guest.

Fenton had finished half his drink and both he and Parkhearst had sat down on the floor at the feet of Grainger.

She began to grow quiet now that they were both with her and both drinking. *If everything,* she had said once a long time ago, *could be a garden with the ones you always want and with drinking forever and ever.*

"Do you think you're going to like Fenton?" Parkhearst began again.

"If you want me to, I guess I can," Grainger answered.

She looked at her drink on the table but then evidently gave up the struggle to have it.

"He looks a little like Russell," Grainger said without any preparation for such a statement.

The remark made Parkhearst go a little white because Russell had been everything. Russell had been her first husband, the one who when he died, people said, made her go off the deep end and drink for ten years, to end up the way she was now.

"Only he's *not*," Grainger added. But she added this only because she saw Parkhearst change color. "Nobody could quite be Russell again," she said.

When Parkhearst did not reply, holding his face in a wounded quivering expression, the great woman flared up. "I said, could they, Parkhearst?"

"Just nobody could resemble Russell," Parkhearst said.

"Well, all right, then, why didn't you say that before?" she scolded.

She ignored his contemptuous silence and acted happy. "Russell was the last of any men that there were," she began, turning to Fenton. "He didn't love me, of course, but I couldn't live without him, every five minutes having to touch him or see him coming somewhere near me . . . . "

"That isn't true, Grainger, and you know it. Why do you lie to this boy, making out that Russell wasn't crazy about you? . . . " Then he stopped as he realized how deadly it was going to be ever to get started on Russell all over again.

"Upstairs," he wanted to tell Fenton, "there was that memorial room to him everybody has heard about somewhere but never seen, a shrine to his being, with hundreds of immense photographs, mementos, clothes, and everywhere fresh flowers every day. Grainger herself never went into the shrine, and Negro women kept the flowers fresh and the holy places dusted."

"Crazy . . . about *me?*" Grainger shot at him and a look of unparalleled meanness came over her face, so that she resembled at that moment a stuffed carnivore he had once seen in a museum. "Nobody was ever crazy about me. The only reason anybody's here now is I have more money than anybody else in town to slake them."

Parkhearst looked up at the word *slake;* he could not ever remember hearing her use it before.

"Look at them!" she shouted, pointing to the dim figures in the next room. "Nobody was ever crazy about me."

Both Fenton and Parkhearst gazed back at the people in the next room as though to see them, in the greatwoman's word, being *slaked.*

Then her anger subsided, and she gave Fenton a brief oversweet smile. Growing a bit more serious and commanding, she said: "Come over here, Fenton Riddleway."

Parkhearst gave a severe nod with his head for Fenton to go to her.

Fenton had hardly gotten to her chair when she reached out and took his hand in hers and held it for a moment. She laughed quietly, kissed his hand in so strange a manner that the action had no easy meaning, and then released it.

Parkhearst had risen meanwhile and poured himself and Fenton another shot of gin.

"You think I should have more?" Fenton said in a way that recalled Claire.

"Well naturally, yes," Parkhearst said, and trembled with nervousness. The comparison of Fenton with Russell did not augur too well. He felt a kind of throbbing jealousy as well as fear. It was the biggest compliment that Grainger had ever given to any of the men he had brought to her house. He felt suddenly that he had given Grainger too much in giving her Fenton and Fenton too much in giving him to her.

Parkhearst realized with a suddenness which resembled a break in his reason that he needed both Grainger and Fenton acutely, and that if he lost them to each other, he would not survive this time at all.

In the midst of his anguish, his eye fell upon both of them coolly, almost as though he had not seen either of them before. It was outrageous, rather sad, and frightening all at once; not so much because she had a dress that was too fine for royalty and Fenton looked somehow seedier than any living bum, but because something about the way they were themselves, both together and apart, made them seem more real and less real than anybody living he had ever known.

"He's Russell!" Grainger said finally, without any particular emphasis.

"No, he's not," Parkhearst replied firmly but with the anger beginning to come to make his words shake in his mouth.

"He is," she said, louder.

"No, Grainger, you know these things don't happen twice. Nothing does."

"Just for tonight he is," Grainger replied, staring at Fenton.

"Not even for tonight. He just isn't Russell, Grainger. Look again."

"I'm going to have a drink now," she threatened him. Half to her own surprise she saw Parkhearst make no attempt to prevent her. She walked rigidly, balancing herself with outstretched hands, over to the little table, filled her glass with a tremendous drain of the bottle, and drank half the draught at once.

"Grainger!" Parkhearst was frightened, forgetting he had permitted her to get up at all.

"All right, he isn't Russell, then. Or he is Russell. What difference! He can stay here, though . . . . Does he need anything?"

The drink, Parkhearst thought, perhaps has sobered her.

She sat down in the great chair and began staring at Fenton again. Then his clothes at last caught her attention.

"Would you accept a suit?" she began. "One of Russell's suits," the greatwoman said, turning her face away from Parkhearst as though to shield her words from him and give them only to Fenton.

Fenton in turn looked at Parkhearst for a clue, and Park-

hearst could only look down, knowing that Fenton would
never understand the generosity that was being offered, the
giving away of the clothes of the dead young Christ.

"Why don't you go upstairs?" She turned in rage now on
Parkhearst. "Why don't you go upstairs with your jealous
eyes and give him one of Russell's suits?"

As her face lay back in the chair, burning with rage, Parkhearst saw how mistaken he had been about her ever being
sobered up by a drink. At that very moment the musicians
stopped playing the new music for the evening, the hostess
fell over, slightly, upsetting her drink, and then with almost
no noise slipped to the floor and lay perfectly still, her drinking glass near her hand, without even a goodnight, lying
there, as Parkhearst observed, looking a little too much like
Hamlet's mother.

                    ✦   ✦

"We may as well go to my house now," Parkhearst said,
after they had got one of Russell's suits on Fenton.

"What shall we do with my old clothes?" Fenton wondered, looking at them with almost as much wonder now
as other people had.

Parkhearst hesitated. "We'll take them," he said. "This
way."

They went downstairs away from the "shrine" and walked
past the room where Grainger was lying on an immense
silver bed with red coverings. She had her clothes still on.
Parkhearst hesitated near the bed.

"I suppose we should say goodnight to her, in case she's
conscious."

They both stood there in dead silence while Parkhearst
tried to make up his mind.

"Grainger!" he called. Then he suddenly laughed as he
saw the serious expression on Fenton's face.

"She's just out, she won't be up and around for God
knows when," Parkhearst explained in his bored tone.
"When she gets in these states she lies till she gets up or

until they find her. I will have to come over here tomorrow and see how things are . . . . "

Then for the first time since they had been in the "shrine," Parkhearst gave Fenton a more critical look. Russell's suit had been a close enough fit all right; the greatwoman had not been too drunk to understand the relative sizes of the two men, although the trousers were a bit too short in the legs. The suit made a tremendous change, of course, and yet the boy who looked out from this absurdly rich cloth seemed to belong in it, despite the expression of pain mingled with rage imprinted on his mouth. He was a Russell of some kind in the clothes.

Parkhearst gave him a last look directly in the eye.

"My wife will be asleep," Parkhearst told him in a rather cross voice, "but if we speak low, she won't hear us. Anyhow we have to have coffee."

Parkhearst's home was an apartment on the fifth floor of a building that leaned forward slightly as if it would bend down to the street.

"I forgot you had a wife," Fenton remarked, looking at him vaguely. "I never thought of you as married."

"A lot of people can't," Parkhearst admitted. "I suppose it's because I never had a job, never worked."

Parkhearst observed with some satisfaction that this made no impression on Fenton. He believed that if he had said he had murdered someone, for instance, Fenton would have accepted this statement with the same indifferent air.

That, as Parkhearst was beginning to see more and more, was the main thing about Fenton, his being able to accept nearly anything. For one so young it was unusual. He accepted the immense dreariness of things as though there were no other possibility in the shape of things.

A cat came out of the door as they entered the apartment. They proceeded down a long hallway to a kitchen.

"I'll throw your old clothes on this bench," Parkhearst said. Then he began to fumble with the coffee can.

Before he began to measure out the coffee he stopped as though he thought somebody was calling to him from the front of the apartment. Then when he did not hear his wife's voice, he began to boil the water for the coffee.

Fenton put his head down on the tiny kitchen table before which he sat.

"Don't go to sleep, Fenton. You can't spend the night here. My wife would die . . . . And Claire must be worrying about you."

"Not Claire," Fenton mumbled. "I thought I told you that we sleep at different times, on account of the bed being so small, and the bugs and all. There are hundreds of bugs." He began to think of the anguish they cause. "They crawl up and down, sometimes they go fast, and you can never find them when they bite. They stink like old woodsheds."

"Bugs are awful," Parkhearst agreed. "But," he went on, "about Claire. He may not miss you, but is he safe alone?"

"I'm too sick to care," Fenton said, his head on the table now.

"How are you sick?" Parkhearst wondered.

"Inside," Fenton replied, still not taking his head off the table and talking into the wood like a colored fortune teller Parkhearst had once known. "Where your soul's supposed to be," he spoke again.

Parkhearst stared at him.

"If there was a God," Fenton said quickly, raising his head from the table and giving Parkhearst an accusing look, "none of this would happen."

"Oh, it might, Fenton," Parkhearst answered. "You don't think He's all-powerful, do you?"

"Do you believe in Him?" Fenton wondered.

"I don't believe but I'm always thinking about it somehow."

"Do you believe Claire is dying?" Fenton said quickly.

"No," Parkhearst answered.

"I keep seeing him dead," Fenton said.

Parkhearst handed Fenton a cup of coffee. Then he sat down, facing Fenton. They both drank their coffee without continuing the discussion. Parkhearst from time to time would listen intently to see if Bella called to him, but there was no sound, no matter how many times he stopped to listen.

"I want to be dead like a bug," Fenton said and lay his head down on the table again.

"Drink all of that coffee and then I'll get you some more."

Parkhearst watched the thick hair come loose from the head and creep over the table's edge like a strange unfolding plant.

"Is this the first time you've ever been drunk?" Parkhearst's voice came from far away.

"I drink nearly all the time," Fenton said, and some coffee began to trickle down the side of his mouth. "When I go home," he went on, "Claire will be dead. I will be happy, like a great load has been taken off my neck, and then I will probably fly into a thousand pieces and disappear. I am sick of him just the same, dead or alive. He makes it too hard for me, just like Mama did. Both him and her talked too much about God and how we would all meet at His Throne on the Final Day . . . . Do you disbelieve in the Throne too?" he looked up at Parkhearst.

The writer watched him, silent.

Fenton was watching him also, almost as though from behind his thick disheveled hair.

"Keep drinking the coffee," Parkhearst said in a soft voice. He felt weak lest Bella should get up and see this. Then he began to feel irritated seeing Fenton in Russell's clothing.

"Grainger is an idiot," Parkhearst said.

"Are you in love with me too?" Fenton asked Parkhearst, but the writer merely sat there drinking, as though he had not heard.

Fenton did not say any more for a long time. Perhaps ten

minutes passed this way in the silence of the city night; that
is a silence in which although one cannot really say *this is
a sound I am hearing now,* many little contractions and
movements like the springs of a poorly constructed machine
make one feel that something will break with a sudden crash
and perhaps destroy everyone.

Fenton knocked his cup off the table and it broke evenly
in two at Parkhearst's feet.

"What did you think of the *church* Grainger has for
Russell?" Parkhearst said, getting up for another cup.

He poured coffee into the cup and handed it to his friend.
"Drink this."

Fenton half sat up and gulped down some more of the
coffee.

"Did you hear what I asked about her *church* for him?"
Parkhearst began again.

"Why did she love Russell so?" Fenton asked, and the
whites of his eyes suddenly extinguished his pupils so that
he looked like a statue.

"He was nothing," Parkhearst said. "Rather beautiful. His
mind worked all right, I guess. He was nothing. He had so
little personality he looked all right in all kinds of clothes.
I think he had millions of life insurance policies. He was a
blank except for one thing. He loved Grainger. I think
maybe he was the one started calling her by her last name,
and now nobody calls her by her first. Grainger didn't love
him, but he told her he loved her every ten minutes. It was
funny, I could never figure it out, why he loved her. I used
to stare at him to try to understand who he was. I think I
know who Grainger is, but not Russell. Then he died in
his car one night. Nobody knows what from. They said his
heart. And he had all these life insurance policies. He was
rich though before, owned factories and mines and patents
and things. After that Grainger never had to think about
work. But I think she's spent nearly all she has. When she
has spent the last of it she will have to die too . . . . "

Parkhearst's voice ended with a little sound like an old

phonograph record stopping but still running. He had not given the speech for any reason except the pleasure he took in telling it. "The way they find him in the car is so beautiful. He had been out drinking all night, and of course he and Grainger together. He said goodbye to her from that car he had from Italy, and she went dragging into her bedroom, not very much like Shakespeare but like the girl in Shakespeare they threw kisses into and out of the balcony, and then Grainger fell down dead drunk on her bed, and Russell still sat out there in the Italian car, trying to call somebody because he suddenly, I suppose, felt sick; the coroner said he had felt sick, Russell had opened his vest, and had blown the horn that only sounded like a small chime (the neighbors told about that), and the next morning there he sat in the sun under her house, dead as time. Grainger never mentioned how he died to anybody we know. She doesn't even drink any more than she did then, but there's something different about her, I guess, because after he died she could never change but always had to go on acting herself."

"The *church*," Parkhearst began again, getting up and looking out into the black windows. "What do you think of the *church*?"

"All those photographs of rich people?" Fenton said.

"Yes," Parkhearst nodded seriously. "And those fake poses of her. She knows she is not the woman in those photos, of course, because she wasn't the woman in her own mind Russell said she was."

"Grainger knows the truth about herself," Parkhearst continued, "but it only makes things more impossible for her. And it's really only money that keeps her alive, and it's going, nearly gone."

"You make me sicker than I was," Fenton said suddenly. "Why do you find out all these things about people when they are so sad?"

"I don't know," Parkhearst said softly.

"How do you know all these things?" Fenton said almost desperately. "Do you know about me like that too?" He lay his head down on the table and didn't wait for Parkhearst's answer.

Parkhearst said nothing.

Then Fenton got up. "I got to go back."

"Where?" Parkhearst was curious and anxious.

"The ALL NIGHT THEATER."

"Why don't you tell me about the ALL NIGHT THEATER some time?" Parkhearst asked.

"There ain't nothing to tell. It's what it says, it goes on all night."

"It's like the park then." Parkhearst had a very quiet voice.

Fenton did not say anything, drinking his coffee from the saucer.

"It's morning," Parkhearst announced more cheerfully.

"You can't tell when it's morning in a city place," Fenton said.

"You told me that before," Parkhearst said, "but that is only because you're Fenton that you think that."

⸗   ⸗

The next day, Parkhearst woke up with a headache and the feeling of rags on his tongue. He knew without looking that Bella had gone to work.

He thought of the greatwoman almost at once and before he thought of Fenton. He would have to go to see her at once. She would still be unconscious, the wreck of her evening undisturbed yet by the maids.

His face looked old and thin and brown in the looking glass, old for twenty-nine. Yet how old did that look, except older than Fenton Riddleway?

Then all the part about Grainger and Russell and Russell's resembling Fenton or Fenton's resembling Russell came back.

"I suppose in Grainger's mind," he said aloud to himself, "she thinks she has already taken him over, away from me. Of course it's true, I've given her everybody she ever had."

He had forgotten Russell only because he had never counted him.

✐   ✐

A not unusual thing was to smell flowers in front of Grainger's house. Today their perfume was stronger than usual. There was the silence of early day inside of the house, but there was evidence that the maids had come and gone, and noiselessly enough to have left her still sleeping in the front parlor.

The flowers, he noticed, were only roses. Grainger lay on the divan, a queer frayed silk coverlet over her. A tiny smile covered her mouth.

"Is the Queen of Hell conscious?" he said in a voice that struggled with both eagerness and contempt.

He began kissing her on the eyelids. "Open those big blue eyes."

Grainger opened her eyes, her smile vanished, and the accusing frown returned. "You cheap son of a bitch," she said groggily. "You never loved Russell. You never even would talk about him. You didn't understand his greatness. His going never even moved you."

"Shall I make you some breakfast now?" he wondered.

"You hated Russell."

He kissed her fingers.

"You make me sick. You cheap son of a bitch," she said, looking at him kiss her fingers. "I ought to hate you. Russell hated you. He said you were lacking in the fundamental. That boy you dragged here last night, what's his name? . . . "

Parkhearst told her.

" . . . he hates you too. You know so damn much. You sit around seeing things so that you can write them down in a hundred years."

Parkhearst went on holding her fingers as though he were giving her the energy to go on.

He looked longingly at some hot coffee on a nearby table,

then letting her hands fall slowly, he got up and went over to the table and poured himself a cup and began sipping.

"And why do we all love you, though, when you stink with cheapness, dishonor, not having probably one human hair on your body. Maybe I love you the most . . . . "

"Don't forget my wife," he said, and the expression *my wife* as he said it had a different quality than that of any other husband who had ever said the words.

"*Your wife!*" she said, getting up and staring at him. "She owns you, but I wouldn't call that loving. Anyhow, she's overpaid . . . . "

"Overpaid?" he said, his mouth dropping slightly.

They were both silent, as though even for them frankness had overstepped itself.

"What was I saying to you when we ran into this quiet period?" she began again.

"About my wife getting too much for her money," he said exhaustedly.

"Who is this Fenton?" she changed topics. "What did you bring him here for?"

"I thought he would be a change for you. You really ordered him anyhow, and have forgotten it."

"I never ordered *him*," she said carefully, drawing the silk coverlet up to her eyebrows. "Did you think he would remind me of Russell?" she put the question with coy crafty innocence, and he felt he would laugh.

"No, Grainger, it didn't occur to me at the time."

"Don't lie to me as though I were your wife!" she lashed at him. "If he hadn't looked a *little* like Russell would you have brought him here then?"

"Yes, I would, Grainger." He smarted now under her attack. "I brought him here because he was so much just himself. This boy is better than Russell," he took final courage to throw at her.

"I'm glad you said *boy*." Grainger was quiet under his blasphemy. "He's a child really. And I'm an old woman."

Parkhearst waited for her.

"How did you find him?" she went on, muttering now, less irritation in her voice.

"How do I find everybody?" he said, a kind of dull bitterness in his voice.

"I never find anybody at all," she said. "Are you jealous because I did something for him?" she wanted to know suddenly.

"Yes, I suppose," he said. "But after all I wanted to bring him here. I was willing to take the risk."

She saw the flowers for the first time.

"Do you know why I buy all these flowers?" she asked him.

"Of course," he said, impatient at her always changing the subject so abruptly.

"No, you don't," she said with a ridiculous emphasis. "Tell me why I have them then, if you know . . . ."

"Why do you have that church upstairs?" he said.

"Church?" she said, somewhat distracted and looking at him with her back to the window. He had forgotten that this was his private word and that he had not ever used it for her; and yet he had employed it with such force of habit, she knew it was his word and that he must say it all the time when out of her presence.

Recovering from her shock over the word, she began to talk about the flowers again: "I can see now you don't know everything after all."

"If there hadn't been any Russell, of course you wouldn't have flowers," he raised his voice as he would have had he lived an ordinary domestic life with ordinary people.

"Should I go to see him?" She changed to a new line of thought.

He stared at her with almost real anger.

"Should I return his call or not?" she roared. "Don't start being Christ with me again or something will happen."

"It's too silly even for you to say," he told her. "Returning a call to Fenton." His voice, though, softened a bit.

"He is very beautiful, isn't he?" she said. "More than Russell was."

"Grainger, you know we never agree with one another about who is beautiful or who is anything."

"He's more beautiful than Russell," she went on, both musing and commanding. "But there's something not right with him that Russell never had. There was nothing really wrong with Russell."

He looked up briefly at her as though something important had finally been said.

"When should I go visit him?" she asked him eagerly.

"We can't go today." Parkhearst acted bored. "Bella's coming home this afternoon from work."

"I wish you would quit mentioning Bella," she complained. "It's all you talk about . . . You get me involved with this new boy, and then you go off with your wife, and leave me without anything."

"Grainger, don't be a complete idiot all the time."

"*I'll* go," she said. "You'll stay home and entertain that Bella and *I'll* go. And every minute," she vituperated, "you'll be thinking of me and him together."

Parkhearst laughed a little, and then the pain of the scene which she had just presented to his imagination bore down with unaccustomed weight.

"You don't even know where he lives," he said. "I can just see you going in there in your finery."

He laughed such a nasty laugh that Grainger found herself listening to it as attentively as one of the "concerts."

✦   ✦

The next thing Fenton remembered was standing in front of a wrestling arena known as Fair City. He was in front of a little wooden gate with his hands put through the partitions as though asking somebody for an admission ticket. It was still early morning, almost no one was on Sixty-third Street; and so removing his hands from the partitions at last, he began walking in the direction of the house.

Right in front of the house he stopped. He heard several voices singing something vaguely sacred. "It's niggers," he said peevishly, rubbing the back of his neck. He raised his eyes to the COME AND SEE RESURRECTION CHURCH. He leaned his head then gently over onto the pavement so that it was within a few inches of the curb and some of the coffee he had drunk came up easily. Then he got up and unlocked the door to the house and went inside.

He felt he must look creased and yellow as he opened Claire's door.

Claire was sitting on the kitchen chair but hardly glanced up at Fenton and only nodded in answer to his brother's greeting.

The sound of the colored spiritualists was just faintly audible here.

"How can they shout when it's morning?" Fenton asked, and then as Claire did not say any more, he asked, "I don't suppose anybody called?"

Claire merely stared at him.

"Ain't you all right?" Fenton said, going over to the chair and touching him.

"Dooon't," the boy cried, as though he had touched him on a raw nerve.

"Claire! Are you sick?" Fenton wanted to know.

"Don't touch my head," Claire told him, and Fenton took his hand away.

"Let me get you into bed, and I'll go for coffee and rolls," Fenton told him and he helped him into the cot.

"I don't want none," Claire said and he closed his eyes.

"You didn't notice my new clothes," Fenton complained.

"Yes, I did," Claire replied without opening his eyes.

"Do you like them?" Fenton said, looking around, as though to find some part of the room that would reflect his image.

"Kind of, yeah," Claire answered.

"I'll go for something for you now," Fenton encouraged him, but he didn't go. He kept staring at the deep pallor of

Claire. He looked around the room as though there might be something there that would extend help to them.

Fenton looked at himself as he sat there on the chair in his new clothes. He wondered if he was changing; there was something about the wearing of those clothes that made him feel almost as if his body had begun to change, that his soul had begun to change into another soul. A new life was beginning for him, he dimly recognized. And with the new life, he knew, Claire would be less important. He knew that Claire would not like Grainger or Parkhearst and would not go to visit them or be with them. He knew that Claire actually never wanted to leave this room again. He had come to the last stages of his journey. Fenton tried not to think of this but it was too difficult to avoid: Claire had come as far now as he could . . . . There could be no more journeying around for him. And Fenton knew that as long as Claire was Claire he would not let him lead the "new life" he saw coming for him. There would be trouble, then, a great deal of trouble.

He wanted desperately to be rid of Claire and even as he had this feeling he felt more love and pity for him than ever before. As he sat there gazing at Claire, he knew he loved him more than any other being. He was almost sure that he would never feel such tenderness for any other person. And then this tenderness would be followed by fury and hatred and loathing, so that he was afraid he would do something violent, would strike the sick boy down and harm him.

"Claire," he said looking at him in anguish. "What are we going to do about this?"

Claire moved his closed eyes vaguely. "Don't know," Claire replied.

Fenton smiled to think that Claire did not ask what *this* was. Well, the boy was past caring, and it was plain enough what *this* was: *this* was everything that faced and surrounded them. It was plain, all right, what it was. Their trouble had made them both one.

"What do you want me to do?" Fenton said, his desperation growing. "Tell me what to do."

"We can't go away now, can we?" Claire said, and his voice was calmer but weaker.

Fenton considered this, taking out from his pantscuff a cigarette butt which he' had begun in the greatwoman's house, lighting it swiftly with a kitchen match, and inhaling three powerful drags all at once.

Claire opened his eyes slowly and stared at his brother, waiting for the answer.

"No, we can't go away anywhere," Fenton said.

"Isn't there any place to go but here?" Claire asked.

"This is as far as we can get. Anyhow for the winter . . . . We have to stick in here now."

Claire closed his eyes again.

"Unless, of course, you want to go and live at Grainger's with me," Fenton said.

"What would I do there in her big house?" Claire said angrily, his eyes opening and closing.

"She would get a special room for you, where you could do anything you want. She could buy you anything you want, take you anywhere and show you anything. You would never know how happy you could be."

"What are *you* going to do there?" Claire wondered with surprise . . . .

"I'm going to marry her."

"Marry?" Claire sat up briefly in bed, but his strength could not hold him up, and falling back flat, he uttered: "You're not old enough."

"I'm more than old enough," Fenton laughed. "You've seen me enough times to know that. I got to make use of what I have, too. She thinks I look like her old husband."

"I ain't going to go there . . . . I ain't going to leave this house," Claire said.

"Well, suit yourself," Fenton said. "But I'm going over there . . . . The only thing is I don't believe any of it. It's a dream I keep having. Not one of those real pleasant dreams you have when you open a package and something beautiful falls out. In this dream even bigger more wonderful things seem like they're going to happen, getting married to a rich woman and living in a mansion and dressing up like a swell and all that, but at the same time it's all scary spooky and goddamned rotten . . . . "

"It's rotten, all right," Claire said. "You don't have to tell nobody that twice."

"Well, when there ain't nothing else you got to stoop down and pick up the *rotten*. You ought to know that."

"Not me. I don't have to pick it up if I don't want to."

"Well, then you can stick here till you choke to death on it," Fenton said passionately.

They both stopped as if listening to the words he had just said. They contained enough of some sort of truth and the truth was so terrible they had to listen to it as though it were being repeated on a phonograph for them.

"When do you aim on going?" Claire said suddenly, his voice older and calmer.

"In a day or so," Fenton warned him.

"Well it could be sooner . . . . You don't mind if I just stay here, do you?" Claire implored him.

"There's nothing to stop you staying here, of course," Fenton said irritably, twisting the hair around his ear. "This house don't have no owner, no tenants, nobody going to bother you but the spooks." He hurried on, talking past the pain that registered on Claire's face when he heard the words. "But I ain't coming dragging my ass over here every day just to see how you are when you could be living like a king."

"You don't need to come over and see me on account of I ain't asking you to," Claire said.

"Well, then don't be sorry if something happens to you . . . . "

"Nothing ain't going to happen and you know it," Claire shouted. "Why would anything happen to *me?*"

"Well, that's because you don't know nothing about cities is all," he said. "Do you know how many murders are done right in this one town?"

Claire did not answer for a moment and then said, "Those

are rich people they murder. Like that old woman you're going to move in with. She's a likely murder person now. And you too if you get to be her husband."

"That's where you're wrong," Fenton said. "Most of the murders they do in this town are on bums, young boys and men that don't have no home and come from nowhere, these they find with their throats cut and their brains mashed out in alleys and behind billboards. Damned few rich people are ever found murdered in this town."

"You think you can scare me into moving into your old woman's house, don't you?" Claire said. "Well, you can do to her all you want to, but I ain't going to be there to watch you . . . fuck her."

"Now listen to that dirty-mouthed little bugger talk, would you. What would Mom think if she knew her religious little boy talked like a cocksucker?" He slapped Claire across the face . . . "after all I done for you," Fenton finished.

"Go be with that old woman, why don't you, and leave me alone," Claire warned him. "I don't need you nor her. I don't need nobody."

"You'll come bellyachin' around trying to get in touch with me, you'll come crawling like you always do some night when you get the shit scared out of you in this house, hearing the sounds that you can't explain, and maybe *seeing* something too . . . . "

Claire could not control the look of terror that appeared at Fenton's words.

"Claire," Fenton changed suddenly to a tone of imploring, "you got to listen to reason. You *can't* live in this old house alone . . . . Something *will* happen to you. Can't you see that . . . . "

"Why will it?" Claire said, his terror abating a little, searching in himself for some secret strength.

"Things happen here. Everybody knows that. Now listen, Claire," Fenton went on, "Grainger would be very good to you and you could be happy there with her, you don't know how happy you would be. You haven't ever been happy or comfortable before so you don't know what you're talking about. Anyhow, Claire, I can't leave you here. I can't leave you here . . . . I'd have to do something else first . . . ."

"I don't see why not," he said. "I would rather be dead than go there."

"You would not rather be dead. You're a tough little bastard and you would rather be alive and you know it . . . . I'm not going to leave you here, Claire. I'm going to take you with me and you may just as well make up your mind to it now . . . . Hear?"

"You won't even get to drag me because I'm not going . . . . "

Fenton's anguish grew. He knew he could not leave Claire and he knew Claire's determination would be hard to break. He felt suddenly an uncontrollable urge of violence against this puny, defiant, impossible little brother. If he had only not taken him from West Virginia in the first place. Or if he had only died as the doctor had said he would a long time ago. He knew that he *did* want to go on to the "new life" with Grainger and Parkhearst. He wanted to change, he wanted to wear Russell's clothes, he wanted the life that was just in sight and which Claire was now preventing. He knew that as long as there was Claire, whether he went with him or stayed in the house hardly mattered, because he knew that as long as there was Claire there was part of his old life with him, and he wanted to destroy all that behind him and begin all over again. Claire was a part of his old life, part of his disbelief in himself, the disbelief he could ever change and be something different. Claire did not even believe he could be married and love a woman. And though Claire was younger, he could exert this terrible triumph of failure over him.

Whether Claire stayed in the old house or followed him to Grainger's, he would exert a power of defeat over him.

Then suddenly Fenton realized that he did not want Claire to come with him. He preferred him to stay in the old house. And at the same time he knew that if he stayed he would never have a moment's peace . . . .

There was no way out that he could see. He could only stand there staring at Claire wtih impotence and rage.

"All right for you," Fenton said at the end. "All I can say is watch out, watch out something don't happen now to you."

✦   ✦

A tent production of *Othello* was to take place that night near Sixty-third Street, the young man who had approached Fenton was telling him, and as somebody was following him he would welcome Fenton's company and protection.

"Who is Hayden Banks?" Fenton wondered, looking at the handbill which described the dramatic spectacle about to take place.

"Hayden Banks," replied the young man, "is one of the greatest living actors. You are probably seeing him just before he is to gain his international reputation. London is already asking for him. Few actors can touch him. He is playing, of course, Othello himself. The costumes are by a friend of mine, and I will introduce you to a good many of the cast, if you like."

"I don't know if I want that," Fenton said.

"You *will* go with me to the performance," the young man said.

Fenton did not say anything. He had to go somewhere, of course, there could be no doubt about that.

"I wish you would come with me because I'm afraid of the man who is following me. Don't look back now. You see, I'm in trouble," he explained. "You look like a good kind of bodyguard for me and if you come with me I'm less likely to get into . . . trouble . . . . And I can't disappoint Hayden Banks. This is the last night of *Othello,* but I have been afraid to go out all week because this Mexican is following me. I'm in awful trouble with him."

Fenton half turned around but he saw nobody in particular behind him, a crowd of people who all seemed to be following them.

"I'll go with you," Fenton said. Then he looked at the young man carefully. He was the most handsome young man he had ever seen, almost as beautiful as a girl in boy's clothes. He had never seen such beautiful eyelashes. And at the same time the young man looked like Grainger. He might have been Grainger's brother. He almost wanted to ask him if he was Grainger's brother, but of course Grainger could not have a brother . . . .

"You don't know what it is, being followed."

"What will he do if he catches you?"

The young man stared at him. Fenton could not tell whether he was telling the truth or making this up, but there was a look of fear on his face that must be genuine at least.

"I wish you wouldn't use the word *catch*," the young man said.

"Are you afraid he will . . . hurt you," Fenton changed *kill* to *hurt* before he spoke.

"I'm afraid of the worst," the young man replied. "And you'll be an awfully good boy to come with me."

Fenton nodded.

The young man signalled a taxi and, waiting, said, "Those are awfully interesting clothes you have on. I've never seen clothes like that before. They remind me of some pictures of my father, wedding pictures."

Fenton looked down at himself as though seeing the clothes on himself for the first time. "These are clothes of a friend of mine," he explained.

"Get in," the young man urged as the taxi pulled up beside them. "Get in and don't stare at the crowd like that."

"Was I staring?" Fenton said, like a man awakened from sleepwalking.

"Staring into the crowd like that might incite him. You have an awful look when you stare," the young man said, looking more carefully now at Fenton. "I hope I am going to be safe with *you* now. I don't usually pick up people on the street like this. And maybe you don't like Shakespeare." He began to examine Fenton now more carefully that he felt free of danger of being followed.

Fenton could see that his anxiety was genuine, but even so the way he said things seemed womanish and unreal, a little like Parkhearst. Both these men said things as though nothing was really important except the gestures and the words with which they said them. When he listened to either this young man or Parkhearst, Fenton felt that the whole of life must be merely a silly trifling thing to them, which bored them, and which they wanted to end, a movie they felt was too long and overacted.

"What is your name?" the young man said suddenly.

Fenton told him and the young man replied, "That is the most interesting name I have ever heard. Is it your own?"

Fenton looked down at his clothes and said it was.

"My name is Bruno Korsawski," he told Fenton.

They shook hands in the dark of the taxi and Bruno held Fenton's hand for many seconds.

"You may have saved my life," Bruno explained.

Soon they reached a vast lot deserted except for a giant circus tent before which fluttered, propelled by a giant cooling machine, banners reading HAYDEN BANKS THE GENIUS OF THE SPOKEN WORD IN OTHELLO. In addition to the angry puffing face of Hayden Banks on the posters was a picture of a rather old looking young man dressed, as Fenton thought, like a devil you might expect to see in an old Valentine, if Valentines had devils, but he lacked horns and a tail.

Fenton remembered vaguely of having read *The Merchant of Venice* and he had heard from someplace that Othello had to do with a black man who tortured a white woman to death. He felt a vague curiosity to see Hayden Banks, however. There was nobody around the huge empty tent tonight, and the whole scene reminded him of the conclusion of a county fair which he had seen in West Virginia.

*   *

Bruno Korsawski was the kind of man who introduced all of his new friends to all of his old friends His life was largely a series of introductions, as he was always meeting new people, and these new people had to be introduced to the old people. His idea of the world was a circle, a circle of friends, closed to the rest of men because of his world's fullness. He had thought that Fenton would be one of this circle. However, the introductions did not go off too well.

They went at once to the star's dressing room. A purple sign with strange heavy tulips drawn on it announced MR. HAYDEN BANKS.

"You dear!" Hayden cried on seeing Bruno. "You look absolutely imperial."

Mr. Hayden Banks did not really look human, Fenton thought, and it was not only the deformity of his makeup.

"This is my friend Fenton Riddleway."

Mr. Banks bowed, and Fenton could not think of anything to say to him . . . .

"Don't you love his name?" Bruno said to Mr. Hayden Banks.

"It's incomparably the best I've heard," Mr. Banks replied. "Uncommonly good. But you've got to forgive me now, I haven't put on my beard yet, and without my beard I'm afraid some of you may mistake me for Desdemona."

"It's been so charming seeing you." Hayden Banks held out his hand to Fenton, and then whispering in Fenton's ear, he said, "You charmer you."

Fenton again could not think of anything to say, and in the hall Bruno said angrily to him, "You didn't open your mouth."

"I guess I'm used to people who talk well and a lot," Bruno explained apologetically as they went to their seats, which were in the first row. "You see what influence can do for you." Bruno pointed. "The best seats: compliments of Hayden Banks."

A small string orchestra was playing, an orchestra which Bruno explained was absolutely without a peer for its interpretation of the Elizabethan epoch. "They stand untouched," he stated, still speaking of the orchestra.

Whether it was the nearness of the actors or the oppres-
sive heat of the tent or the general unintelligibility of both
what the actors said and what they did, Fenton became
sleepy, and he could not control a weakness he had for break-
ing wind, which considerably upset Bruno, although nobody
else in the small audience seemed to hear. Perhaps Fenton's
slumber was due also to the influence of the ALL NIGHT
THEATER, and drama for Fenton was a kind of sleeping
powder.

When Hayden Banks made his appearance, there was a
tremendous ovation from the first few rows of the tent, and
for a while Fenton watched this tall bony man beat his chest
with complete lack of restraint and such uncalled-for fury
that Fenton was amazed at such enormous energy. He could
think of nothing in his own life that would have allowed
him to pace, strut and howl like this. He supposed it belonged to an entirely different world where such things were
perhaps done. The more, however, the great Moor shouted
and complained about his wife's whoring, the more sleepy
Fenton became. It was, however, something of a surprise to
hear him fret so much about a whore and have so many rich-
looking people nodding and approving of the whole im-
probable situation.

"He kills Desdemona," Bruno explained, watching Fenton doze with increasing displeasure.

"Would you buy me a drink now?" Fenton asked Bruno
during intermission.

At the bar, the bartender asked Fenton if he was old
enough, and Bruno said, "I can vouch for him, Teddy," and
exchanged a knowing look with the bartender.

"There is one thing," Bruno began to Fenton after he
had nodded to literally scores of friends and acquaintances:
"I wonder if you couldn't control yourself a little more during the soliloquies at least."

Fenton knew perfectly well to what Bruno referred but
he chose to say, "What are those?"

"During the performance, dear," Bruno went on, "you're

making noises which embarrass me since I am among friends
who know me and know I brought you as a guest."

"My farts, then?" Fenton said without expression.

"Brute!" Bruno laughed gaily.

"Would you buy me another whisky now?" Fenton asked
him.

When they returned to their seats Fenton immediately
dozed off and did not waken until the last act which, whether
due to his refreshing sleep or to the fact the actors seemed to
talk less and do more, was rather frighteningly good to him.
Hayden Banks seemed to murder the woman named Desdemona (Aurelia Wilcox in real life) with such satisfaction
and enjoyment that he felt it stood with some of the better
murder shows he had seen at the ALL NIGHT THEATER. He
applauded quite loudly, and Bruno, smiling, finally held his
hand and said, "Don't overdo it."

After the performance, Bruno invited Fenton to meet the
entire cast, and as drinks were being served now in the
dressing room, Fenton drank four or five additional whiskies
to the congratulations of nearly all present. At times Fenton
would have sober moments and remember Aurelia Wilcox
patting his hair or Hayden Banks giving him a hug and kiss,
or the young man who played Iago and who looked even
more like a Valentine devil off the stage whispering in his
ear.

"Hayden says we're to go on to his apartment and wait
for him there," Bruno explained finally to Fenton, showing
him at the same time a tiny key to the great man's rooms.

✓   ✓

"You were extremely rude to Hayden Banks. You act like
a savage when you're with people. I've never met anybody
like you. What on earth *is* West Virginia if you are typical?"

They were in Hayden Banks' apartment and Fenton, instead of replying to Bruno's remarks, was looking about,
comparing it with Grainger's mansion. The walls had been

painted so that they resembled the ocean, and so skillfully done that one actually thought he was about to go into water. Fenton stared at the painting for a long while, noticing in the distance some small craft, a dwarf moon and the suggestion of dawn in the far distance.

"Arden Carruthers did that painting," Bruno said. "Arden Carruthers is one of the most promising of the younger artists and this mural will be worth a small fortune some day."

Bruno was smoking something strange smelling which Fenton recognized as one of the persistent odors of the ALL NIGHT THEATER. As he smoked, he drew nearer to Fenton, and his expression of critical disapproval of the boy suddenly vanished.

"What are you clenching your fists for, as though you were going into the prize ring?" Bruno said.

Fenton sniffed at the cigarette and then suddenly knew what it must be. It was what had changed Bruno.

"You are very beautiful looking. The Italian Renaissance all over again in your face," Bruno said. He kept standing right over Fenton as though he were a bird that was going to come down on top of his head. He kept staring right into the crown of his head.

Fenton suddenly reached out and with violence seizing Bruno's wrist cried, "Give me some of that," so that the cigarette nearly fell from his fingers.

"Have you ever had any?" Bruno wanted to know.

"Give me some," Fenton said again, remembering now with terrifying insistence the smell in the ALL NIGHT THEATER. He felt that he could really dominate this man now as much as he could Claire. At the same time he was terribly afraid. He felt that something decisive and irrevocable was about to happen.

"Just smoke a little of it and don't inhale as deep as I did," Bruno said nervously. "I don't think you know how."

Fenton took the cigarette and began inhaling deeply.

"Now stop," Bruno said. "I don't have a warehouse of those."

"No wonder somebody was following you," Fenton laughed.

"I wonder which one of us is more scared of the other," Bruno said finally, and he sat down at Fenton's feet.

Fenton was about to say that he was not afraid of anybody, but Bruno began babbling about Fenton's shoes. "Where on earth did you get *those?* They're privately manufactured!" He stared at Fenton with renewed respect and interest. "You didn't get *those* in West Virginia."

Bruno stared at Fenton again.

"You haven't killed anybody, have you?" he said finally.

Fenton stared at him and he went on agitatedly, "Why, you've finished that entire cigarette. I hope you know what you've done and what it was. I'm not responsible for you, remember."

"Who the fuck is responsible?" Fenton said.

"Don't use that language," Bruno sniggered, and then got up swiftly and sat down beside Fenton. He began kissing his hair, and then slowly unbuttoning his shirt. He took off all his clothes, as from a doll, piece by piece, without resistance or aid, but left on at the last the privately manufactured shoes . . . .

The next thing Fenton remembered he was standing naked in the middle of the room, boxing; he was boxing the chandelier and had knocked down all the lamps, he had split open Bruno's face and Bruno was weeping and held ice packs to his mouth.

Then the next thing he remembered was Bruno standing before him with Hayden Banks who looked exactly like the murdered Desdemona. Bruno had a gun in his hand and was ordering him to leave.

"Don't you ever come back if you don't want to go to jail," Bruno said, as Fenton went out the door dressed in clothes that did not look like his own.

*   *

Morning is the most awful time. And this morning for

Fenton was the one that shattered everything he had been or known; it marked the limits of a line, not ending his youth but making his youth superfluous, as age to a god.

He seemed to be awake and yet he had the feeling he had never been awake. He was not even sure it was morning. He was back in the old house, in Claire's room, and though he was staring at Claire he knew that his staring was of no avail, that he already knew what had happened and the staring was to prevent him from telling himself what he saw. He could not remember anything at that moment, he had even forgotten Bruno Korsawski and the production of *Othello* starring some immortal fruit.

Then the comfortable thought that it was breakfast time and that he would go out and get Claire his rolls and coffee. He was so happy he was here with Claire and he realized again how necessary Claire was to him, and how real he was compared to the Parkhearsts and the Brunos and the Graingers.

Claire, he said softly. He went over to the bed and began shaking him. The room seemed suddenly deadly cold and he thought of the winter that would come and how uninhabitable this deserted old wreck would be . . . . And Claire, he recognized, almost as with previous knowledge, was as cold as the room. And yet he was not surprised . . . .

He sat there suddenly wondering why he was not surprised that Claire was cold. And at the same time he was surprised that he could be so cold. He shook him again.

Claire, he said.

He began to be aware of a splitting headache.

He got up and turned on the sickly light. He was careful somehow not to get too close to Claire now that he had turned on the light, but stood at a safe distance, talking to him, telling him how he was going to get him some breakfast.

"Some good hot coffee will make you feel like a new boy, Claire," he said.

And then suddenly he began to weep, choking sobs, and

these were followed by laughter so unlike his own that he remained frozen with confusion.

"I'm going right now, hear?" he said to Claire. "I'll be right back with the coffee . . . . " Then he laughed again. The silence of the room was complete.

He hurried to the lunch stand and then ran all the way back with the steaming coffee and rolls.

He bent down over Claire but was somehow careful not to look at his face. His head ached as though the sockets of his eyes were to burst. He kept talking to Claire all the time, telling him hqw they were going back to West Virginia as soon as he got a little money saved up; they would buy a stock farm later and raise Black Angus cattle, and have a stable of horses. It was not impossible, Claire, he said.

He held Claire's head up but still without looking and tried to pour the coffee down his throat. "This coffee's strong enough to revive a stiff," he laughed, ignoring the coffee's running down the boy's neck, ignoring that none of the coffee had even got into his mouth.

"Eat this bread," he said and put some to Claire's mouth. He pressed the small piece of roll heavily against the blue lips, smashing it to the coffee-moistened cold lips.

"Eat this, drink this," Fenton kept saying, but now he no longer tried to administer the bread and coffee. "Eat and drink."

We have to go back, Claire. We want to go back to West Virginia, you know you do.

Then as though another person had entered the room and commanded him, Fenton stood up, and pulled the light down as far as he could to search mercilessly the face and body of Claire.

The light showed Claire's neck swollen and blue with marks, the neck broken softly like a small bird's, the hair around his neck like ruffled young feathers, the eyes had come open a little and seemed to be attempting to focus on something too far out of his reach. The brown liquid of the coffee like blood smeared the paste of the offering of bread around his mouth.

Fenton looked down at his hands.

After that he did not know what happened, or how long he stayed in the room, trying to feed Claire, trying to talk to him, trying to tell him about Black Angus in West Virginia.

Slowly the sound of Fenton's own voice worked him from the stupor he had been in, saying again and again, "You're dead, you little motherfucker. Dead as mud and I don't have no need sitting here staring you down."

＊   ＊

For a good many days he walked all over the city, riding street cars when they were full so that he could shove his way in without paying, eating in cheap lunch stands when they were full and running out the back door without paying the bill. He found he could steal fruit and candy from grocery stands without much trouble. In the evening he would go to the Square in front of a large gray library and listen to the revivalists and the fanatics.

Older men sometimes invited him to a beer, men he met in the crowds in front of the speaker, but as he drank with them his mind would wander and he would say things which chilled further talk, so that after awhile absently he would look around and find himself alone looking down at his hands.

There was no respite for his misery during which time he slept in hallways, covering himself with newspapers he collected in alleys. By day he would go down to the docks and watch crews unload cargo, or he would go into a large museum where they kept the bones of prehistoric animals which he knew never existed. These big-boned monsters calmed some of his crushing grief.

But at last there came to him an idea which gave him some solace, if not any real hope or restoration. It was that Claire must be put in a sheltered place. He must have a service, a funeral. The thought did not occur to him that Claire was really dead until then; before he had only thought how he had killed him. And the thought that anybody *knew* he had killed Claire or was looking for him never occurred to him. What had happened to both him and Claire was much too terrible and closed in for the rest of the world to know or care about.

It was night when he returned to the house. He had vaguely remembered going upstairs weeks before and finding an old chest up there, an old cedar chest, perhaps, or merely an old box. He walked up the stairs now, using matches to guide his way. He heard small footsteps scamper about or it might have been only the echo of his own feet.

He stood in the immense vacant attic with its suffocating smell of rotting wood, its soft but ticklingly clammy caress of cobwebs, the feeling of small animal eyes upon him and the imperceptible sounds of disintegration and rot. How had he known there was a chest up here? As he thought of it now he could not remember having seen it. Yet he knew it was here.

He put himself on hands and knees and began groping for the presence of it. He came across a broken rocking chair. His kitchen matches lit up pictures on the wall, one of a girl in her wedding dress, another of a young man in hunting costume, one of Jesus among thieves. Another picture was a poem concerning Mother Love. At the extreme end of the attic and in a position which must have been directly above the room where he and Claire had lived and where Claire now lay dead was a chest; it was not a fragrant cedar chest, such as he had hoped, but an old white box with broken hinges and whose inside lid was covered with a filthy cloth.

But even more disappointing was that inside was a gauzy kind of veil, like a wedding veil and his eye turned wearily to the picture of the girl in her wedding costume as though this veil might be the relic of that scene. But whatever the veil was, it might serve this cause. It was not a fit resting place for Claire, but it would have to do.

He hurried now downstairs and into the room, with the sudden fear that Claire might have disappeared. He sat

down beside him, and his agony was so great he scarcely noticed the overpowering stench, and at the same time he kept
lighting the kitchen matches, but perhaps more to keep his
mind aware of the fact of Claire's death than to scare off the
stink of death.

It took him all night to get himself ready to carry Claire
up, as though once he had put him in the chest, he was
really at last dead forever. For part of the night he found
that he had fallen asleep over Claire's body, and at the very
end before he carried him upstairs and deposited him, he
forced himself to kiss the dead stained lips he had stopped,
and said, "Up we go then, motherfucker."